T0299058

JOHN JENNINGS: CONVERSATIONS

Conversations with Comic Artists M. Thomas Inge, General Editor

John Jennings: Conversations

Edited by Donna-lyn Washington

University Press of Mississippi • Jackson

The University Press of Mississippi is the scholarly publishing agency of the Mississippi Institutions of Higher Learning: Alcorn State University, Delta State University, Jackson State University, Mississippi State University, Mississippi University for Women, Mississippi Valley State University, University of Mississippi, and University of Southern Mississippi.

www.upress.state.ms.us

The University Press of Mississippi is a member of the Association of University Presses.

Copyright © 2020 by University Press of Mississippi
All rights reserved
Manufactured in the United States of America

First printing 2020
∞

Library of Congress Cataloging-in-Publication Data available
LCCN 2020014574
Hardback ISBN 978-1-4968-2938-2
Trade paperback ISBN 978-1-4968-2939-9
Epub single ISBN 978-1-4968-2940-5
Epub institutional ISBN 978-1-4968-2941-2
PDF single ISBN 978-1-4968-2942-9
PDF institutional ISBN 978-1-4968-2943-6

British Library Cataloging-in-Publication Data available

Works by John Jennings

The Hole: Consumer Culture: A Graphic Novel Vol. 1 by Jennings and Damian Duffy (2008)

Out of Sequence: Underrepresented Voices in American Comics, curated by Jennings and Damian Duffy (2009)

Black Comix: African American Independent Comics, Arts and Culture, creative directors Jennings and Damian Duffy (2010)

Black Comics: Politics of Race and Representation, coedited by Sheena C. Howard and Ronald L. Jackson II; book cover art and design by Jennings (2013)

Mothership: Tales from Afrofuturism and Beyond, edited by Bill Campbell and Edward Austin Hall; book cover design by Jennings (2013)

Pitch Black Rainbow: The Art of John Jennings (2013)

Afrofuturism: The World of Black Sci-Fi and Fantasy Culture by Ytasha Womack; book cover art and design by Jennings (2013)

Black Kirby: In Search of: The Motherboxx Connection, coedited by Jennings and Stacey Robinson (2013)

Black Queer Identity Matrix: Towards an Integrated Queer of Color Framework, edited by Sheena H. Howard; book cover art and design by Jennings (2014)

The Hip Hop Underground and African American Culture by James Braxton Peterson; book design by Jennings (2014)

Kid Code: Chapter Zero by Damian Duffy; illustrated by Jennings and Stacey Robinson (2014)

The Liminal War by Ayize Jama-Everett; book cover design by Jennings (2015)

The Entropy of Bones by Ayize Jama-Everett; book cover design by Jennings (2015)

Stories for Chip: A Tribute to Samuel R. Delaney, edited by Bill Campbell and Nisi Shawl; book cover design by Jennings (2015)

APB: Artists Against Police Brutality: A Comic Book Anthology, contributor, cobook design (2015)

The Blacker the Ink: Constructions of Black Identity in Comics and Sequential Art, coedited by Jennings and Frances Gateward (2015)

Graphic Design for the Curious High School and College Students: Why Study Graphic Design?: The Undecided Student's Guide to Choosing the Perfect University Major and Career Path by Dr. K. Vaida; chapter "Strategic Thinking in Graphic Design" by Jennings (2015)

Blue Hand Mojo: Hard Times Road, story and art (2016)

Prison Industrial Complex for Beginners by James Braxton Peterson; illustrators Jennings and Stacey Robinson (2016)

I Am Alfonso Jones by Tony Medina; illustrators Jennings and Stacey Robinson (2017)
Kindred: A Graphic Novel Adaptation by Jennings (artist) and Damian Duffy (2017)
The Encyclopedia of Black Comics, edited by Dr. Sheena Howard; book cover art and design by Jennings (2017)
Latinx Superheroes in Mainstream Comics: Latinx Pop Culture by Frederick Luis Aldama; book cover design and foreword by Jennings (2017)
Cosmic Underground: A Grimoire of Black Speculative Discontent, coedited by Jennings and Reynaldo Anderson (2018)
Black Comix Returns, creative directors Jennings and Damian Duffy (2018)
Sunspot Jungle Volume One, Volume Two, edited by Bill Campbell; book cover art and design by Jennings (2018)
Box of Bones (10 issues), cocreated, coillustrated, and cowritten by Jennings and Ayize Jama- Everett (2018–2020)
Emergence Magazine.Org Myrtle's Medicine by Kinitra Brooks; illustrated by Jennings (2019)
Bitter Root (Issues 1–5) by David F. Walker and Chuck Brown; back matter "Bitter Truths," curated by Jennings (2019)
Bitter Root: Red Summer Special by David F. Walker and Chuck Brown; back matter "Bitter Truths," curated by Jennings (2019)
Megascope publishing graphic novel imprint, curated and directed by Jennings (2019–)
Reflection Eternal: The Candyman Illustrated Syllabus, featuring the artwork, design, and pedagogy of Jennings, Stacey Robinson, and Damian Duffy (2019)
The Paradox of Blackness in African American Vampire Fiction by Jerry Rafiki Jenkings; book cover art by Jennings and Stacey Robinson (2019)
Afrofuturism Rising: The Literary Prehistory of a Movement by Isaiah Lavender III; book cover art by Jennings and Stacey Robinson (2019)
Is'Nana the Were-Spider: The Ballads of Rawhead and John Henry by Greg Anderson Elysee; *Ringing True: Ballads, Rhymes and the Creation of History*, essay and back cover art by Jennings (2018)
Parable of the Sower: A Graphic Novel Adaptation by Jennings (artist) and Damian Duffy (2020)
Parable of the Talents: A Graphic Novel Adaptation by Jennings (artist) and Damian Duffy (forthcoming)

CONTENTS

INTRODUCTION

Born November 5, 1970, in Mississippi, John Ira Jennings considers himself an artist above everything else. His introduction to the comic book world was early and led him to a career in which he's able to explore aspects of what it means to be human through art. By the same token, in cultivating, amassing, and preserving art through several means, Jennings is someone who understands what an education can help you do. He acquired his bachelor's degree in 1993 at Jackson State University. In 1995, he received his MEd in media arts education and in 1997 a MFA in studio and graphic design at the University of Illinois at Urbana-Champaign. Similarly, he shares his knowledge. He has taught at SUNY University at Buffalo as associate professor of graphic design and visual studies, the University of California at Riverside as professor of cross cultural studies, and at the University of Illinois in hip hop design. Jennings has also been a Nasir Jones Hiphop Studies Fellow at Harvard University. His love of comics, education, and teaching has also led to his being the cofounder and organizer of the Schomburg Center's Black Comic Book Festival, located in Harlem, New York; the MLK NorCal Black Comix Arts Festival in San Francisco, and SOL-CON: The Brown and Black Comix Expo at Ohio State University. Jennings has also coedited the Eisner award-winning *The Blacker the Ink: Constructions of Black Identity in Comics and Sequential Art*; *Cosmic Underground: A Grimoire of Black Speculative Discontent*; and *Black Comix Returns*, which features independent writers, artists, and conventions focused on black culture.

In several of his interviews Jennings discusses W. E. B. Du Bois and the influence of horror in his work, as well as growing up in Mississippi. Much of his art explores and deals with the historic trauma of black and brown people in the United States. In several interviews he pointedly discusses Martin Luther King Jr. as being an Afrofuturist. Mostly this is done by Jennings pushing and, at times, bypassing the boundaries of the comic book medium. Showcasing the underrepresented in comic books, Jennings unapologetically confronts racism and a mixture of stereotypes and misperceptions that ignores the humanity of black people (for example, focusing on the lynching of Emmett Till in Mississippi). In essence, art should matter; particularly, black people and people of color should see in the things they consume (comic books and graphic novels, specifically) reflected back at them. Artwork should represent the microcosm of people within a society. All the good, bad, and ugly of it. Jennings is someone who has seen a need for the artistic unrepresented within the comic book world and has done something about it. His work attempts to defy stereotypes of African Americans, through a variety of methods. Throughout his career Jennings has been using the comic book/graphic novel medium to bring the marginalized to the forefront of their narratives. In a sense he reclaims this through an industry cluttered with supermen and wonder women. Instead of traditional heroes Jennings creates characters who they sell half their souls to the darkness in order to avenge their families.

One gets the sense when reading the solo works or collaborations Jennings has been involved in that he's not interested in elitists who sit in some imaginary high tower, reading dead white men who write about the problems of dead white men. Rather he wants to challenge systemic racism, white supremacy, and the denial of seeing mankind in people by drawing and developing characters that may not look like typical superheroes. He does this through his art and writing without apology. Specifically, in the anthology *APB: Artists Against Police Brutality*, first co-created as a Facebook page, and later as coeditor and contributor, Jennings shines a light on institutional racism and what artists attempt to do to combat it. The anthology is filled with images of black and brown men and women dealing with police brutality and various forms of terrorism. However, each short story, personal account, essay, and comic illuminates how and why the lives of people of color continue to be devalued based on the color of their skin.

Likewise, Jennings is a man who successfully blends cultural heritage, politics, and the legacies of slavery into his narratives. Because he is a black man, there are some things he does not have to research or attempt to figure out. Also, unlike what often happens to black writers and artists in corporations, Jennings does not have management forcing Caucasian characters on him for fear of alienating white audiences. More importantly, comic books have a pulse. They are living and usually in the moment. Yes, there is a considerable amount of planning involved. By the time you get those pages in your hand, know that a culmination of artists, writers, and editors have been working on those storylines for months. Comic books do not just happen; at the same time they can respond to what is occurring in the world right now. As an educator, collaborator, curator, creator, writer, and artist Jennings takes this into consideration.

When it comes to comic books, they enable us to understand the times we are living in. They are spaces where we can examine our place in the world or engage in fantasies free of punishment. We cheer for the hero or root for that marginalized individual who achieves those small victories. We may even nod our head in agreement when someone is just going through a normal day and they nearly get sideswiped by falling debris. Jennings does this through his writing and specifically his artwork—most notably with Damian Duffy, a longtime collaborator. Jennings and Duffy have worked on a series of projects together, including *The Hole: Consumer Culture Volume One*, which explores consumerism and racism in inventive ways, and, more recently, the graphic novel *Kindred*, adapted from Octavia Butler's 1979 novel, followed up by adaptations of Butler's other novels *Parable of the Sower* and *Parable of the Talents*. Jennings has also created characters who previously had lingered on the fringes of mainstream comic books. His creations, specifically works where he has been the creator, writer, and artist, allow him to make a space which shows a spectrum of experiences beyond the stereotypes often used in comics. For example, in Jennings graphic novel *Blue Hand Mojo: Hard Times Road* his protagonist is not an ex-con (though he does work with criminals). Instead his past is violent for different reasons. He and his family are lynched. Somehow he reaches out to the black noire, a possible incarnation of the devil, and survives. He spends his time in depression era 1930s Chicago, helping friends through powerful gray magic, at times for a rather large price—sometimes monetary. He is what is known as a conjurer, a rootworker who uses supernatural forces to increase his abilities. His magic is also practical. It helps his dark-skinned, black girlfriend pass for white to make a living. The way Jennings portrays the world his protagonist moves in is complex, thought-provoking, and riddled with black people of various shades and ages. It is a world where magic is used to deal with racism, in a real and practical way. No one has a cape; still Jennings is creating superheroes.

Yes, literature employs many ideas and theories; however, we need stories that should be reachable—the most accessible place being comic books. That is what comics and graphic novels can do, help people make connections. They continue to assist us in understanding what is happening in the world and give us a reference point we may not have had before. The work that Jennings does makes him a forerunner in a forum where people of color, and, more specifically, those of African/Caribbean descent can be kings and villains in the same narrative. There is a standard now. It is not enough to be a face in the background.

When I was growing up all I knew were DC and Marvel Comics. I did not dream about comics with characters as strong as the ones I read in books. As an adult, when I read *Kindred* in graphic novel form, I felt compelled to reach out to Duffy but, more importantly, to Jennings. In the world of social media and as an educator I was able to ask them about their research processes and what did they read growing up. The visceral reaction of seeing Dana in their adaptation of Octavia Butler's novel do all the things I imagined in my head traumatized me to the core. Her stature, haircut, and especially her skin color shook me. I did not know what to do with all my feelings. In not having to use my imagination I cried through the entire graphic novel. I saw myself for the first time ever. Dana looked like me. She was not some disproportionate, young male's wet dream. She was a real person confronting an impossible problem. But she was also smart and capable—and had all the attributes of what can be considered a superhero. John Jennings did that. He made a hero who looked like me. Explaining his work helps me pull back the layers of his artistry and allows me to see connections with continual societal problems that may not be recognizable at first read in other forms of literature. Essentially, that is the motivation for this book. There's an emptiness in academic study that is filled by Jennings's teachings and constant exploration of humanity through his art and collaborations.

The interviews compiled in this volume begin with a conversation that discusses the evils of copyright and the love of hip hop. Other interviews go into the influence of Jack Kirby on Jennings's perspective of what art can do, the collaboration of Black Kirby with Stacey Robinson and his love of horror, from Stephen King to Edgar Allan Poe, as well as the films *Candyman* and *Us*. Jennings also goes in-depth into the importance of comic books in academia and his favorite comic book character, as well as why and how *Blade* began the success of Marvel comic book characters moving from the comics to movies. What I want others to understand about Jennings's work as a comic artist is to show how essential his craft has been to reshape how comic books are perceived. Equally as important is Jennings being from Mississippi and his mother's and grandparents' influence on not only his art but his approach to teaching, which is essential in understanding the necessity for his being widely known.

I'd like to thank the publications and interviewers who gave their permission to be included in this volume. But I would especially like to thank John

Jennings for his contributions, patience, advice, and, most of all, art. Reading his interviews have given me a deeper appreciation of teaching and reminder of what comics are able to do.

DW

Frank "Half-Man" Johnson, the protagonist of the graphic novel *Blue Hand Mojo: Hard Times Road*, from *Pitch Black Rainbow: The Art of John Jennings* (2014). © 2019 John Jennings, permission of John Jennings.

CHRONOLOGY

1970	John Ira Jennings is born in Brookhaven, Mississippi.
1988	Joins the military but discharged shortly thereafter due to an injury.
1993	Graduates from Jackson State University with a BA in art.
1995	Graduates from the University of Illinois at Urbana-Champaign with a MEd in media arts education.
1997	Graduates from the University of Illinois of Urbana-Champaign with a MFA in studio and graphic design.
2001	Becomes an associate professor of graphic design at University of Illinois at Urbana-Champaign.
2008	Receives tenure and becomes a professor at University of Illinois at Urbana-Champaign. *The Hole: Consumer Culture Volume One*, a disturbing horror/science fiction tale which looks at consumerism, is published by Front Forty Press. It is one of the many collaborations between Jennings and Damian Duffy.
2009	Collaborates with Duffy on *Out of Sequence: Underrepresented Forces in American Comics*, which explores the art of over sixty artists from diverse backgrounds, genders, ethnicities, and sexual orientations in the medium of comics and the use of sequential art. Wins a Glyph Award for *The Hole* for rising star in independent publishing.
2011	Becomes an associate professor of art and visual studies at University at Buffalo SUNY.
2012	Contributes illustrations to the comic-strip *BlackJack: Heart of Evil* (twenty-seven episodes)
2013	Collaborates with Stacey Robinson on *Black Kirby: In Search of the Motherboxx Connection*, published by Rosarium Publishing. Both he and Jennings utilize the art of artist Jack Kirby to reshape the narrative to reflect the black experience. Curates art exhibition The Motherboxx with Robinson, which contains essays from academics

of varying backgrounds on the artwork and what it represents. *Pitch Black Rainbow: The Art of John Jennings* is collected in one anthology and published by Rosarium Publishing.

2014 *Kid Code: Channel Zero*, a hip hop–time travel adventure story is published by Rosarium Publishing. Jennings marries.

2015 *APB: Artists Against Police Brutality*, published by Rosarium Publishing, shines a light on institutional racism and what artists attempt to do to combat it. *The Blacker the Ink: Constructions of Black Identity in Comics and Sequential Art*, coedited with Frances Gateward is published by Rutgers University Press.

2016 *The Blacker the Ink* wins the Eisner Award for Best Scholarly Work in Comics. It also wins the Ray and Pat Browne Award for Best Edited Collection in Popular Culture and American Culture by the Popular Culture Association/American Culture Association. Wins the PEN Oakland–Josephine Miles Award for Excellence in Literature. *Blue Hand Mojo: Hard Times Road* is published by Rosarium Publishing.

2017 *Kindred*, the graphic novel based on Octavia E. Butler's 1979 novel of the same name, is published by Abrams ComicArts. Jennings illustrates while Duffy adapts the written narrative. *Kindred* is the winner of the Bram Stoker Award for Superior Achievement in a Graphic Novel given by the Horror Writers' Association. It is also the last graphic novel to be number one on the *New York Times* bestseller list for graphic novels before the list's disbandment. Co-illustrates *I Am Alfonso Jones*, published by Tu Books. Jennings is awarded the Nasir Jones Hiphop Fellow at Harvard University.

2018 Becomes professor of media and cultural studies and faculty member in the Department of Creative Writing at University of California Riverside. *Cosmic Underground: A Grimoire of Black Speculative Discontent*, coedited with Reynaldo Anderson, is published by Cedar Grove Books. *Black Comix Returns* is updated and published by Lion Forge. *I Am Alfonso Jones* is YALSA's top ten graphic novels for teenagers. Jennings creates the course Afrofuturism and the Visual Cultures of Horror at University of California Riverside. Jennings wins the gold from PubWest for *The Encyclopedia of Black Comics* Best Book Design. Jennings and Duffy win the Eisner Award for Best Adaptation from Another Medium for *Kindred: A Graphic Novel Adaptation*. The short story "It Could've Been," written by Frederick Luis Aldama with art by Jennings is published. Co-creates with Stacey Robinson the art exhibition Uncaged: Hero for Hire, which debutes at University of California Riverside and examines the importance of Marvel Comics' character Luke Cage.

2018–2020 The first few issues of *Box of Bones*, a comic book maxiseries co-created, co-illustrated, and co-written by Jennings and Ayize Jama-Everett is published.

2019 Jennings becomes curator of his imprint Megascope, which is part of Abrams ComicArts. Co-creates a syllabus with Robinson and Duffy entitled Reflection Eternal: The Candyman Illustrated Syllabus, featuring artwork, design, and pedagogy based on the horror movie *Candyman*. Son is born.

2020 *Parable of the Sower: A Graphic Novel Adaptation*, adapted from the Octavia Butler novel of the same name, is published by Abrams ComicArts.

2021–2022 *Parable of the Talents: A Graphic Novel Adaptation*, adapted from the Octavia Butler novel and follow-up to *Parable of the Sower*, to be published by Abrams ComicArts.

JOHN JENNINGS: CONVERSATIONS

Fantastic Blackness with John Jennings

RAYMOND MORALES / 2012

From *The Show*, hosted and produced by Raymond Morales, MD, PhD, November 13, 2012. Reprinted by permission of Raymond Morales. Originally published on *Black Kirby Now: An Interview with John Jennings*.

Raymond Morales: Good evening folks. Thank you for tuning in; we have another fantastic evening of *The Show*. We have an amazing broadcast coming forward. We're going to have a good time this evening; as always we're going to have an amazing conversation. Politics and bullspit and in the process we're going to bring to the forefront an illustrious artists.

Go ahead and tell them who you are, where you come from, and give them a little spiel about yourself, okay?

John Jennings: My name is Professor John Jennings. I teach now at the University of Buffalo in the department of visual studies, and, basically, I'm a graphic novelist and social justice kind of entrepreneur to a certain degree. I make stories about black people and about their struggles and graphic novels, so that's what I do. I'm also a curator.

RM: You know if you're someone who loves artwork, comic book art or any graphic novel work, you should be a fan of John Jennings. I feel that they are all amazing work. So you touched on the fact that you're a graphic novelist, first let's start talking about your career. Let's talk about what you're working on now, we'll talk about how you got there, and then we'll jump to the future. So what are you working on right now?

JJ: I appreciate that. Thank you, right now I'm working on this this new comic called *Blue Hand Mojo*, which is basically a narrative about a Mississippi conjure man and is set in the 1930s, like the Depression Era. And, basically, it's kind of a southern gothic tale to a certain degree, but it's dealing with the great migration, the numbers game, and also looking at the black body as kind of a haunted space. It's dealing with this idea that I call the "Ethno-Gothic" where you're dealing with the revenants of slavery and discrimination, which kind of followed black people to Chicago and other spaces as they migrated up north. I actually got a humanities fellowship from the University of Buffalo to work on this project, so it's very exciting. So in the spring I'm basically going to be working on a new graphic novel about this.

RM: So they're going to like pay you to draw.
JJ: It's like the University of Buffalo is subsidizing this graphic novel to a certain degree. So basically, the Humanities Institute is kind of like how the IPRH is at the University of Illinois where scholars apply for monies to buy themselves out of the contracts to work on a research project. And so, I think I might be the first artist to get one there. But you compete against anthropologists and historians and what have you to get this opportunity. It is quite an honor actually, so it feels good to be supported in the work.

RM: You actually showcased some of your work; actually you showcased a snippet of it I believe in tonight's lecture.
JJ: That's correct—some of the beginning pieces of it. Yeah, I mean, I've been working on this story for about a year now. It was a collaborative piece at first, now it's just me working on it, and it's grown and changed over the last year. And I think it's in a good space now. I mean, I really am excited about the piece. Something else I'm working on right now is this collaboration with a *really, really* talented writer Nnedi Okorafor, who is a winner of the World Fantasy Award for best novel [2011]. Her book is called *Who Fears Death*. It's like a postapocalyptic, sci-fi narrative, that's set in sub-Saharan Africa; it's beautiful. But the piece I'm working on for her is a short story called "On the Road," and it's kind of like a . . . it's not so much unlike the sort of stuff that I do. It's about this woman who's haunted by her ancestors because she's not really living up to a full potential, and it's like a wake-up call for her. She's a Nigerian American character and what happens in the story is this weird thing that happens to her on the road where she's basically changed by this experience. So I was honored to be working on this peace with Nnedi. I'm adapting it into a graphic novel for her.

RM: That is dope.
JJ: I'm really excited about that project. We've been working on it for about a year, give or take, and you know, I'm changing some things with it. But you know it's really exciting to work on it with her. She's a very talented woman.

RM: Yeah, and it's crazy. You've only mentioned two actual projects, but really you have so many arms that you're not even . . .
JJ: Yeah, I mean, it's like, you know, I'm working on curatorial projects. I have a new piece that I'm working on with Stacey "Black Star" Robinson called Black Kirby, which is touring right now. It's a show of our own work which is about eighty-five objects that we generated over the summer. And it's looking at the intersections between Jewish American creators and Black American creators. But it's also an Afrofuturistic, black-power fantasy piece. So, it's dealing with these social justice issues, its dealing with empowerment through entrepreneurship, and it's dealing with black history. It's like a mishmash of a lot of different things. It's beginning to get some really good feedback from critics and stuff, and it's travelling. And we actually do it with self-publishing a catalog through Create Space.

RM: Feel free to talk louder so that some people can actually hear you.
JJ: Oh, am I not talking loud enough? I'm sorry.

RM: Nah, I was just playing. But in terms of Black Kirby, people may not know that you're referencing Jack Kirby. Who is that for people who are new to the comic world, who may not be familiar with his work? They should. I mean they're familiar with his work. But they're not familiar with Jack Kirby.
JJ: Stacey and I got this idea because, well, the first thing I was working on was this show with Dr. Adilifu Nama, who's a professor at Loyola Marymount University, and he wanted to do a show about the black independent experience in comics. And so we did a show called Fantastic Blackness and so when he said Fantastic Blackness, I said, oh, Fantastic Four. So I actually used the typeface which is used for *The Fantastic Four* which is a Marvel comic that was created by Jack Kirby and Stan Lee in the 1960s. It's one of the first, like, major Marvel . . . right, it was like the DNA.

RM: Right.
JJ: And so we started flipping some of the characters.

RM: Yes.
JJ: Because we started flipping these Marvel characters, these Jack Kirby characters into black characters. So like Captain America became Major Sankofa.

RM: Like some of these that are here. [Morales is referring to the artwork being showcased in the background where the interview is taking place].

JJ: Yes, or like Big Barda from *Mister Miracle* [DC Comics] becomes Big Sister. You know, stuff like that.

RM: The Hulk . . .
JJ: Yeah, so like the Hulk became the Buck. [Laughter] So this is where it kind of started from. And so then what happened is that Jack Kirby's family actually sued, or tried to sue, Disney for remuneration for some of his creations. Look at some of the characters that he created. He co-created Captain America. He co-created Thor, Iron Man, the Silver Surfer, and Galactus. He had just a pantheon of characters. They call Marvel the house that Jack built, right?

RM: Right.
JJ: So then we started thinking; we start thinking about the connections between some of the things the Jewish creators were going through. For instance, the idea of a passing narrative. You know, because a lot of the creators would change—either the creators were changing their names, like his [Jack Kirby] real name is Jacob [Giacobbe] Kurtzberg and Stan Lee is Stanley Lieber. You know, that kind of idea. And there were a lot of Jewish creators who basically couldn't get better jobs because at the time comics were considered such a low medium. But they changed the landscape of the pop culture, kind of like the experience in America, and inspired a lot who are African American who are working in what we call the Black Age of Comics movement. So, that's what we got this idea of Black Kirby from. So the show is called Black Kirby Presents: In search of the Motherboxx Connection. We're looking at the connections between, like, funk, you know, and this idea of Afrofuturism that comes from this musical tradition.

RM: Mm-hmm.
JJ: But then looking at stuff like the fact that Jack Kirby co-created the Black Panther before the Black Panther party actually started.

RM: Which makes you wonder.
JJ: Yeah, it does. I mean, you know, so we would like to make any connections more explicit, like X-Men, which is obviously about otherness and was kind of like made in the encounter of what was going on in the civil rights movement in looking at those characters and how they could be reflecting Dr. King and Malcolm X. Like that kind of piece. So we just made those more explicit and just started remixing things. We put in a lot of hip hop. We put in science fiction. We put in all kinds of stuff, you know, just black power politics and

looking at how those things have been depicted. So that's where Black Kirby came from. So the mother-box was this idea that Jack Kirby had where it was a living computer that connected to the source, which of course is a reference, which we look at as a reference, a reference to the hip hop magazine, you know.

RM: Yes, right.
JJ: So we were like, Hey, the mother-box connection, the mothership connection. We just started making this piece. Oh, and the fact that the source is this blank wall, which is basically what this hand of fire writes on. So it's almost like cosmic graffiti. We were like, This is perfect. It just started mixing up just perfectly. So Black Kirby is kind of like Gnarls Barkley where it's like two people joining together to become one. It's a really cool way to talk about double consciousness, too. So we started playing with those theories and stuff. And we made, like, eighty-five artifacts over the summer, and people like it.

RM: Some of it is very striking. We saw some of the images already. But I think the story you're getting at in terms of Jewish artists during that period of time and even scholars in general if you look at some of the early other forms and, for example, in Vaudeville, we spoke earlier about the Three Stooges, right? And how, I think, it was Columbia Tristar pictures that basically abused them. I forgot who their manager was at the time who basically paid them on a for-hire basis, sort of as a consultant. Yeah, you know, once their work was done, that's all the money they're going to get.
JJ: And that's what happened to Jack Kirby. Definitely, and a lot of artists too.

RM: It's a story that goes beyond the years, and the reality is that these artists could have never imagined that they were going to make all these digital movies. And then go into DVDs, which didn't exist at that time.
JJ: Well, it's like Bill Finger. Are you familiar with Bill Finger?

RM: No, I'm not.
JJ: Bill Finger is the co-creator of *Batman*.

RM: Oh, really?
JJ: So it's not just Bob Kane, the artist. Yeah, but Bill Finger, he was from a poorer family. He was the writer that worked on *Batman* with Bob Kane. Bob Kane came from a more affluent family, and so he was able to protect himself legally. Bill Finger died in poverty. In fact, it's ironic, but it's like they call what happened to him getting the finger. Jerry Siegel and Joe Shuster, the

two Jewish kids at the time who created *Superman* were fired off of *Superman* by DC Comics.

RM: That's horrible.
JJ: I know what happened was horrible.

RM: Imagine, like, your own creation coming back to you; it's like a child coming back to you and slapping you in the face.
JJ: Seriously, and what happened to . . . Neal Adams at the time was working on *Batman*, and he actually got DC; he shamed DC into giving Siegel and Shuster a modest pension because this was around the time that the first *Superman* movie [1978] was coming out. So yeah. Now you have the Comic-book Legal Defense Fund that's out there. And they have funds for artists who have fallen on hard times and stuff because it just what's going on in the comics industry.

RM: Yeah, and it's really crazy when you think about how that story extends to so many other forms, like Grandmaster Flash and the Furious Five and some of the other artists who don't get any remuneration for their work because again once their work was done and what some of the labels do to some of their artists. You know there are very few artists or MCs who actually fulfilled their legal contract because sometimes they require you to do ten albums. It's like a ridiculous amount of work you need to pull off to have to fulfill a given contract.
JJ: Yes, yes. That's right.
RM: So you've gone through some of your work right now. How did you get to this point because people out there may not realize? Like they think, I want to be an artist or whatever; they don't think it's possible to become successful make a living off of it. Tell people how you got to that point.
JJ: Yeah, you know my main gig is I'm a professor right, so that's the thing. I'm a tenured professor. It's funny because I was at San Diego Comic Con this past summer and I was speaking on a panel with Keith Knight. And Keith Knight, who's actually in the *Black Comix* book referred to my professoring [sic] as a side-hustle [laughs].

RM: Look there goes the fist in the background [referring to the slide show of artwork behind them].
JJ: Yeah right, because his piece was you have to do what you have to do to make the comics. So [Keith Knight says] you have people like John, he's like your side hustler. He's a professor, but he's a comic book artist. So I went to

school, and I started drawing at a very young age. I mean, I started drawing as a young person at like four or five years old, and I fell in love with comics at an early age as well, like around ten or eleven. I always wanted to be a comic book artist. And then it's been a really weird journey. I ended up in the military at first when I was like around seventeen. I went into the army because, well, because even though I was valedictorian and I was good at art, no one told me that I could actually be an artist. I really didn't have that access and it freaked me out, so everyone went into the military. So what am I going to do? Oh, I'm good at art. Then I had an accident though and so it messed my foot up. I actually have a piece of steel in my right foot. Yeah, yeah, open reduction and internal fixation.

RM: Oh wow.
JJ: Yeah, they call it peace-steel. So . . .

RM: It's a very nice word for that.
JJ: Yeah, its peace steel painful. [laughs] Yeah, so I ended up getting a scholarship to Jackson State University where I majored in commercial art, which is the great-granddaddy of graphic design, you know, still wanting to be a comic book artist but realizing that it's a very competitive field at the time. And you know it still is of course. You would think to be in the field of comic book artists you would have to move to New York. Because at the time, this is like pre-internet. It's people FedExing their stuff; you know, that kind of thing.

RM: And to get a job for . . .
JJ: Exactly, so I went to art school. I thought I was going to be an illustrator. I ended up working for a newspaper right out of school [called] the Clarion-Ledger, which was a Gannet paper. And I really enjoyed working [there]. I liked it a lot. But I got a chance to go to grad school here at the University of Illinois. And I took that chance. I didn't know what was going to happen, I didn't know what I was getting into, but I took a chance and started growing a lot. As a grad student my professors pushed me into doing comics, thank God. Because at the time *Understanding Comics* by Scott McCloud was out, and some people were starting to pay attention to the form of comics as a medium—and so just like, serendipity. So that's why I got back into comics. And I started looking at the new forms and at the time you had stuff like Milestone Media [the black-owned comic imprint of DC Comics] coming out; Valiant [comics] started. Vertigo [the supernatural-mature audience imprint of DC Comics] started in the early nineties as well, like *Sandman* and *Hellblazer*. *Hellboy* started in the

nineties too. And so that's what got me back into it. I started around 1992, yeah, but anyway so that's what got me back into it. And then when I went back to Jackson State I started their graphic design program pretty much and worked there for, like, four years and was recruited back to University of Illinois at Urbana-Champaign to help with the image-making aspects of the graphic design program. And then I fell into doing research on identity and comics and hip hop, looking for different intersections between masculinity and hip hop, and how it's performed in popular media. And I started looking at hip hop, comics, and wrestling, and seeing these connections, I just fell into doing comics again. So then I met Damian Duffy, and we started doing these crazy social justice–oriented comics and trying to sell them. And before you know it we are curating shows on identity and comics, and you know, then here we are. Yeah, seriously, and so now I'm, like, you know, the guy who does black comics. You know it's weird. Yeah, so that's the truncated story of how I ended up in this area. So now I'm a comic book artist. It's crazy.

RM: What's interesting is that I recall a conversation I had. It's still very vivid for me when I was younger where my music teacher caught me reading one of my comic books in school. And she basically just chastised me in saying that comic books had no place in school, that I couldn't learn from them. And I really, in the moment, I just snapped on her. I said what are you talking about?
JJ: You have no idea. You don't know nothing. [laughs]

RM: No, but I was really taken aback by her because it's like she had never taken the time she was just in a superficial valley. Because if you read comics you would know there was more than just that layer of the artwork. Because the artwork, even though it could be beautiful, could make social commentary on pop culture, but also the dialogue could also be powerful. The words that they use. Because you know if you're a young kid and sometimes you can see a big word and the context, it's so much more vivid and is more likely to stick with you and resonate with you when you see Spiderman flipping and doing a backflip through the New York City skyline and using a big word versus reading it in a 2-D book, and there's other words crowding it and hiding its meaning doesn't stick out to you.
JJ: That's a really good point.

RM: So that for me was really problematic in terms that some people just don't get it.

JJ: Yeah, we're still thinking that we live in, like, this logo-centric world where words are the only thing we need to read. And as you know there are different types of literacies. You have social literacy, historical literacy, computer literacy. This is a multimodal-literary world that we live in. Images are always joined with pictures these days because of things being marketed to us. One thing that always irks me is people think about comics as a gateway to real reading; you know, that kind of thing . . .

RM: Like how marijuana is to real drugs.
JJ: Right, and so the whole thing is like, now, comics are a totally different way of reading period because they fuse images and texts in a very interesting way. And they're a great way of teaching multimodal-literacy.

RM: I feel like that market, in terms of, like, e-zines is not really tapped into yet. They don't really speak to that venue, that medium. You spoke earlier today on the fact that comics being viewed as being only for children. Whereas if you look at the early history of cartoons, maybe [inaudible] would know this, most cartoons were made for adults. And it's only really in the seventies and eighties you start to see them transition to being for children.
JJ: That's right. There are a lot of different things around comics. Comics have a really trippy history in our country actually because the superhero comics, which were booming during the Golden Age was like 1930s, '40s, post–Second World War; you know, it's like where that kind of ended a little bit, you started seeing these other comics that are about horror or a romance or comedy or celebrities and stuff. But it was really dominated by the superheroes, which were so connected to the Second World War because they would send them to Captain America, who was punching Hitler in the face. Everybody who was creating these superheroes, they were fighting the Nazis. So what happened after the Second World War, people connected those characters to the Second World War; they didn't want to forget about them. They wanted to rebuild America. They wanted to rebuild Europe. So that's when these other forms came along, and then you had this one company called EC Comics which created *Tales from the Crypt*. You know, they were selling like hotcakes—crime comics, horror comics—and moms were pissed off. Then came along a man named Dr. Fredric Wertham, who wrote this book called *Seduction of the Innocent* that was totally vilifying comics. And there was a senate-subcommittee hearing where comics were forced to self-censor. At the same time this is the '50s where you have this new thing called television that was jumping off, and this other new thing called rock and roll. So while these other forms were starting to grow, comics

were being sequestered and kind of vilified. So it really stunted their growth until the '60s where you had underground comics and Marvel Comics and stuff like that. It's really trippy history.

RM: Definitely, I mean we're both big fans of comics and artwork in general. That's why I said for me it's a blessing to have you on here. You see some of the artwork in the backdrop. I know it's not all you've created per se directly. Could you to talk about some of the people you've collaborated with?
JJ: Right now I'm collaborating with Stacey "Black Star" Robinson, who is a really talented artist in graphic design out of Fayetteville, North Carolina. He's part of Tribeca Studios, and he used to do this comic called *Abraham, the Young Lion*. We're working on some stuff together. He's part of Black Kirby; he's like the other half of Black Kirby. So we've been working together on things. Sometimes he will draw original pieces, and I'll color them in the computer. Or we'll sample and remix each other's work, or I'll draw some of it and he colors it. So it's kind of like a passing-back-and-forth-of-the-mic kind of thing from a hip hop perspective. Right now I'm getting ready to color some of Shona Mills's work. Shona Mills is this very gifted artist and illustrator and animator. She actually did some work on a *Black Dynamite* TV show, and we have this piece called *Graffiti Monster Killer* that we actually work on together with Damian Duffy. I should be working with Jeremy Love on a new piece pretty soon called *King Thundered* that I'm really excited about. He's doing the writing and Kenji Marsh—he's a really talented artist out of the Detroit area, and I'm doing the colors on that as well. I did some color stuff with Ashley Woods. She's a Chicago-based artist, and also I'm working with Eric Battle, who's a really super-talented brother who's done work for DC and Marvel. We're trying to get this work together for this calendar that we want to do but also some stories that we want to work on together too. So collaborating, it's like part of what I do now because, I mean, I caught a bug working with Damian. Man, you know, opening it up and working with other people . . . you know we're going to speak with Aaron Monroe too eventually. So yeah, but I have my hands full.

RM: You've only really mentioned two projects, but it's like there were so many more than that.
JJ: It's just really crazy, man. I need to prioritize a little bit more. I have this curse. I have the story curse. I'll wake up with a fully formed story in my head, you know.

RM: And you've got to get it all out.
JJ: So the best way to get that done is to share. You can't keep the ideas to yourself. You have to share the ideas, or they'll just wither and die. But when you start having dialogues about the ideas that's when they become really powerful, you know. It's pretty amazing doing the collaborative thing. You know comics, like art, can be collaborative anyway just because of the nature of how people write them, people draw them, ink them. So they can be inherently collaborative anyway. So it's a great medium to work in. You know, most comics people are really cool people. Seriously.

RM: I'm going to throw a word out there. I want you to react to it, to respond to it. The word is *copyright*.
JJ: Whoa, copyright.

RM: Yeah, let's talk about copyright because we touched on it slightly with Jack Kirby and his efforts where a lot of the first Jewish artists, the way that they were treated, and I guess in many ways abused by institutions that be . . .
JJ: I go back and forth about it because you know I'm really into this idea of the creative commons too. You know sometimes this notion of copyright really kind of hinders the growth of knowledge to a certain degree or freedom of creativity especially if you're looking at people who are working as VJs or DJs or what I call CJs, like myself, who sample things that we see, and you know it can be a hindrance to a certain degree. It does protect the people who are generating it. For instance the copyright law is, like, you create a piece and it's set up in a way that it's automatically copyrighted and that kind of becomes a general law. But it does to a certain degree hinder some creative expression. And there's lots of things we don't have access to that are copy-written. It's like sequestered away from us, that if we had access to it maybe it would open up different dialogues. So, I'm really into this idea of sampling and remixing in my work. I sample and remix stuff all the time.

RM: That's inherently American . . .
JJ: Yeah, that's a lot of what American culture is, sampling and remixing. And we brought all this stuff together as a big mixing board of a country. So I think the idea of privatization of knowledge is kind of scary, but you want to be protected. I think, honestly, that if we weren't in a capitalistic society it wouldn't work; it wouldn't matter because we think about it before we start doing this thing. We had oral culture, right? We were passing along stories

orally, we told each other [stories], and they got passed down. When you start fixing it, copywriting, controlling it, distributing it, the system itself makes it very difficult to hack into it and make your own work. For instance, I think that you know what some people do with manga. There's this elective Japanese manga. They actually have a section that's just for fan-based stories. So yeah, actually, support the fan. You know so people can actually take something that's based off of, like, *Spiral* or something and write their own *Spiral* stories and put them out. And they helped the sales of the *Spiral* comic book. So I think that we should have that kind of thing happening in American comics, in American movies. People want to make this stuff because they love it. So why punish them when they want to love something you're making because you're biting the hand that feeds you to a certain degree. So I go back and forth, but I understand why it's in place. But I really think that at the end of the day we should have access to as much knowledge as possible and that we can make and build things more efficiently if we have access to them.

RM: I like the metaphor you use with hip hop. I remember when I was younger in terms of making mixtapes. I would make my own mixtapes. I would buy them at the newsstand. DJ Clue, DJ Doo-Wop, all these different DJs would have mixtapes at the stores. And it's like if they weren't able to do that, it would hinder . . . I mean that's at the time when obviously they were obviating any sort of copyright law.
JJ: That's pre–*Three Feet High and Rising* that was the album from De La Sol where they really starting cracking down.

RM: There was an era where just the free flow of knowledge and art was so amazing. It got to a level of, I would say, a renaissance, if you will, that we haven't really revisited because then you have these people become basically monopolies and you have these corporations built around people. I can't even sample this work because if I do I have to pay this person and this person and the person to sample them. Come on, that's not the way we make more beautiful art. That's a thing today; that's what I want to see. And it's not to take it away from the artist per se or keep them from having their fair share of recognition. You know money, etcetera, but it's like the object is not to . . . I mean from my advantage because again going to the notion of capitalism, right? It's not about the money you make; it's about making some dope stuff.
JJ: Yeah, I'm with you right there. I mean, have you seen this piece called *Rip Remix Manifesto*? I forgot who the director was, but he talks to Lawrence

Lessig, who wrote that book *Remix Culture* or *Remix*? But he talks about creative commons quite a bit. Girl Talk is one of the people he looks at a lot. And he does a lot of music-making through sampling and remixing. So yeah, it's dealing with these ideas. You know the creative commons is where we do this remix stuff. That's what we do, and that's where we are too as a society. The digital culture allows us to do that. You know everything can be a sample.

RM: Exactly, and it really hurts me to think that it's not as accessible as when we were younger. I mean, it's accessible but not as permissible. So as before, you could make a mixtape for yourself. But if it gets, if it's really good, and then the company finds out you are super screwed. So in terms of your work now, if you could project five or ten years down the line, where would you see yourself—whether it's professionally in an academic setting or into drawing etcetera—what would you be doing, what would you be working on, and where would you be?

JJ: So here's the thing, I've come to kind of, like, a crossroads right now because what's happened is post-tenure; you know, a lot of the work that I'm doing as an artist is catching up with the academic side too. I've been juggling the writing and academic analysis kind of stuff with the artwork. I did not know that Black Kirby would get picked up by different venues. I just did it because I wanted to work with Stacey and it was the proper time to do it. Being a colorist on a major graphic novel or working on pieces that become published joints that get a lot of notoriety, that's starting to happen. I'm thinking that in the next few years I want to fuse those things a lot more. So I'm looking at doing more critical discourse through visual essay. Actually creating art that is more analytical in nature based off of some of the work of what John Berger was doing in his book way back in the '70s where you're juxtaposing images to create a narrative that is about critical discourse. From that standpoint I want to do more of that work. I have a ton of ideas that I want to work on with Damian Duffy and Stacey and other creators in the next few years. I'm going to start focusing on making the work and trying to get it out there in as many ways as possible.

RM: If you could go and check his website or even the Tumblr page I think you all would be amazed and shocked on how dope some of the work is. Just like I said, it's crazy. People know when I first brought him on to *The Show* it actually took me a while . . . I was like hunting him down for months . . .

JJ: I was so busy man. I'm so sorry.

RM: It's all good, man. I totally understand we're on different worlds, and I was grateful when it finally did come through. I was disappointed because we had the whole technical aspects, and even with some of the work we're seeing featured in the back right this is just a small, small sampling of his work. If you go and just peruse, there's just so much more that you're not seeing in terms of the consciousness and also just the flavor from all the things you're sampling. There are just so many elements, and I told them I don't like to see just the image, you know. Sometimes it's about the thickness of the lines; sometimes it's about the font you use. Do you have just an image, or do you box it out? There's much more depth than just that. So I definitely appreciate it. In terms of future scholars who are coming through the ranks, what advice would you have for someone who's thinking about going into this career like you or wanting to pursue something similar?
JJ: I think the artist/scholar model is something that people look at. And I think in the academy we did this with what they call interdisciplinary studies. I mean, it's funny because institutions are institutions because they've been around for so long. It's a closed system to a certain degree, and so I think some of the scholars like myself, like yourself, are finding ways to circumvent those systems because we will find ways to get around those closed systems. And I think a lot more scholars like that are coming in with that mentality. And so crossing the stream—so to speak to kind of borrow from the discursive—how that's right, so this interdisciplinary nature is actually becoming like the norm. That's what's really exciting. So you know at Buffalo, for instance, the visual studies program is pretty much like that, the art history program is fused with the studio program and they became visual studies. So these notions of creating spaces where people can be an artist and a scholar simultaneously, I think that's going to become something that needs to be pushed more in universities. So, I'm thinking, like, embrace it—that if you are a scholar and you're working on these artistic notions of identity and critical analysis to go for it. I think that there's going to be a space for you. That's what I think.

RM: I'm just curious any questions from the folks in the audience; anything you'd like to know or ask John? Anything you would like to ask him? I will ask you this: recently, I had the privilege earlier to win a copy of the dope *Black Comix*. I'm looking at the image, then if you go any sort of old-school comic books, you know that the dopest part of the cover was when you had metallic reflections. I would always get two copies, one with the reflection, and one I would keep in the bag where I would keep it sealed up. I definitely want to say thank you to John for coming on the show. And also if you want to find out

more about the Black Comics Project go to Facebook, which is actually becoming highly acclaimed. Lots of folks, thousands and thousands of folks are flying across the country. For those who aren't familiar with it tell people what that project is because they may not be familiar with it.
JJ: *Black Comix* is a collection of about fifty or so after African American artists who are working with what we call the Black Age of Comics' movement which was basically kind of jumped off by Turtel Onli in Chicago, who actually teaches at Kenwood Academy, since the early nineties, and it's a community of artists who do amazing work underground who just happened to be African American. So Damian [Duffy] and I did this as an offshoot project from some of the curatorial exercises we're doing about identity across the board and stuff. And it wasn't to ghettoize or sequester black artists in a certain way. It's just that we knew that if we brought that to a publisher . . . it hadn't been done before . . .

RM: Which is shocking.
JJ: I know right, but people didn't know they were out there . . .

RM: Or they didn't want to know.
JJ: Yeah, maybe, but they're out there, and so this is the book. And, you know, it's done pretty well. Mark Betty, the publisher, published it for us. Random House is our distributor for it. And it's been selling worldwide actually. And there's a copy of *Black Comix* in the Nelson Mandela library in South Africa. You know stuff like that. I like to track to see where the book goes, like Singapore and the United Kingdom; it's crazy. Yeah, it's crazy. When one of my friends was in England, in London he saw a copy of it in a bookstore. I was like . . .

RM: What was your reaction when you heard?
JJ: That was great. I love it because people are checking it out. And, you know, I think that it's gotten a lot of exposure for these artists who are working tirelessly. We talk about people who are bouncers, and they go and make comics—or they wait tables and go and make comics. You know, they teach like myself and go home and make comics. So it's about the love of the medium; that's what *Black Comix* is.

RM: It's dope, but if you flipped through the book as I started doing today you'll see that there's just so many different styles. It's not just one flavor, I guess we could say, [inaudible] black comics when you go through it. We see many different styles from different inking, coloring, etcetera. And talking about that project—can you talk about what it's like when you have something like this with a hardbound cover versus doing an ease-on because there's something to be said for having it physically with distribution versus having it electronic and digital?

JJ: Yeah, so I teach design history and graphic design history, and it's one of the things that I've been thinking about quite a bit. You have an app like *Comixology*, which is one of the biggest distributors of digital comics right now; they've started outselling *Angry Birds* as the top app. So people are reading comics online. It works really well. It has this thing called guided view where basically what it does is it'll show you the comic in context, you double-tap it, it goes to the individual panels, and it just kind of follows around. What it does is it makes you focus on the comics a lot more. People wrote about it saying, "Wow, this is a really interesting way to read a comic book." I think that's what's going to happen. I could see the comics' medium, it looks so good online, and it's made for it. There's this really good book by this futurist, I'm forgetting his name, but it's looking at San Diego Comic Con and the future of the comics' medium. And it gives, like, ten points that need to happen in order for this to jump off. And one of them is for them to come up with a unifying file format, like an mp3. They need that because what's happening now is that you have to have an app for this and all these copyright things; they need to let that go to PDF. But also you create an app that would do that for everybody so that's one thing about distribution having access to printing on-demand comics. If you could go to something like Create Space you can actually make a nice comic. A brother could profit off a comic and Create Space through something like Amazon because you have an instant digital distribution. You could make a Kindle book, and you could push it through their networks and stuff. For a little bit more you have access to the retailers. Really, it's a viable way to make comics. It's going around the traditional locked-up, closed systems. For instance you have this sixteen-year-old girl who outsold [the graphic novel] *Watchmen* with her book; it's called *How to Be a Supervillain*. It's a kid's book, and she outsold *Watchmen*. She's a bestselling author through Amazon, and she's just sixteen. That's the kind of world we live in, the rise of the prosumer. But you also have the art book itself, like *Black Comix* is an art book—you want that in your hands. I think what's going to happen is that certain things that books do—that focus on the book-ness, the affordances of the medium—that's what's going to happen.

RM: Exactly. You can't get this glossy reflection or flutter. You can't experience some of the artwork; it's just so amazing.

JJ: Exactly, you can simulate it but you can't do that, the texture of the paper, that kind of thing. I just saw this book this evening, the born-again series *Daredevil*, Frank Miller, and it's the one where the kingpin totally destroyed Daredevil. So they just put out this special edition book. David Mazzucchelli, he's the artist on it, he scanned in all of his original artwork at high [resolution], and they made a book that's huge. That is the entire series as a black-and-white comic that shows the eraser marks, his overlays, where he put in the smoke. You can't do that with, you know . . . and I bought it so hard. It's amazing, but I still have *From Hell*, which is a five-hundred-page graphic novel in my book-bag all the time because I don't have it on an iPad. So, I have not stepped foot into a comic book store in many years, in like the last two or three years.

RM: I know same here.

JJ: But I don't have to anymore. Also due to Amazon because basically the different file formats are going to do what they do. You're going to have books that are just for collectors, but you're also going to have . . . I don't want to collect all the *Static Shocks* right now, but I want to read them. I think that's what's going to happen: you're going to have the portable stuff that you just want to do the periodical thing, and then there are works like *Absolute Watchmen*. It's gorgeous. It's huge swollen, big, opulent; that's what the book does. But the media can't do it. I mean, the multimedia can't do it.

RM: I think many comic bookstores have to adapt to that as well because they haven't caught up with that yet. And that's why they're suffering in terms of sales because they're still relying on . . .

JJ: That direct market.

RM: Yeah, they're still relying on supporting the old institutions, the printing masses, which you cannot do. You have to adapt to the times, and they have not done that.

JJ: I think the guy in the book that he wrote, and I forgot the guy, but he said the printing-on-demand aspect—where you just print what you need digitally or want—could save the retail market. It's really smart. But if you have people who are relying on that for money, they're not going to actually let you into that closed system because it's connotative; it's going to bank. They don't really care about the people who are making those books. And then you actually have to sell a certain amount of books to be even part of that market. So once they up the ante for us, like independent comics' artists making their own books, and get into the Diamond distribution system . . . a lot of books are not going

Legba, from *The Hole Consumer Culture: Volume I* (2008). © 2019 Damian Duffy and John Jennings, permission of John Jennings.

to sell fifteen-hundred copies. They might sell sixty copies; they might sell enough to eat. And that's fun but let us do it. But if it's a closed system, then you can't do it so that's why stuff like Haven Distribution is an alternative distribution system to the direct market, but then you have all these other places like Indy Planet, places like that.

RM: Last words and thoughts: what do you want to offer folks out there who are tuning in, watching us?
JJ: You know, I love this quote from James Baldwin, "Artists are here to disturb the peace," so I hope that I disturb it properly. And I urge people to disturb it as well. I want to make work just like that and for other people to do as well.

RM: I'd like to thank John Jennings for coming on the air. I'd like to thank him for sharing his artwork and showcasing the backdrop and also for signing the book. Peace out.

Black Kirby Now: An Interview with John Jennings

JULIAN CHAMBLISS / 2014

From *PopMatters* magazine, February 20, 2014. https://www.popmatters.com/179294-black-kirby-now-an-interview-with-john-jennings-2495685683.html. Reprinted by permission of PopMatters Media, Inc.

John Jennings, associate professor of visual studies, and Stacey "Blackstar" Robinson comprise the collaborative entity that is Black Kirby. The project is an exploration of legendary comic creator Jack Kirby's work through an Afrofuturism lens. A term coined by writer Mark Dery in 1994, Afrofuturism describes a genre that infuses African diaspora sensibilities into science fiction, fantasy, and magical realism frameworks. The resulting creative work explores a pan-Africanism rooted in future realities.

With roots in the political and social tumult of the 1970s, the first stirrings of Afrofuturism are linked to musical artists such as Sun Ra and, to a lesser extent, George Clinton's Parliament Funkadelic. In reality the broader contours of an imagined future free from contemporary limitation allow us to consider deeper historical roots to Afrofuturism. W. E. B. Du Bois's 1920 short story "The Comet," which tells the story of a black bank messenger who emerges from a bank vault to discover he and the beautiful daughter of a wealthy businessman are the only people alive after poisonous gas from the comet's tail kills the entire city, is perhaps the first example of Afrocentric science fiction. Hinting at the taboo subject of miscegenation, Du Bois's story suggests possibilities unthinkable in the public consciousness. In a similar vein, Zora Neale Hurston's work celebrating African American folk culture in works such as *Mules and Men* leverage tall tales and legend to validate an African American culture obfuscated by white society. By exploring the fantastic, Hurston created a context to understand the black experience.

Afrofuturism, then, offers a space for artists, academics, critics, and activists to explore the cultural tension around a future state whereby economic, social, and political anxieties linked to the African diaspora will be resolved. Seen in this light, the 1970s origin resonates with the US domestic experience of African Americans grasping political and economic power in the wake of 1960s liberal activism and global realignment out of the postcolonial reorganization on the African continent.

An Afrocentric future is born out of the inspiration and aspiration of a growing African diaspora. Of course, this promising future is a reflection of a troubled past and contested present. Forever linked to a narratology of a past reclaimed and a present contested, the "future" becomes what Hayden White described as "a realization of projects performed by past human agents and a determination of a field of possible projects to be realized by living agents . . ."(4). Afrofuturism sketches the boundaries in a manner that calls into question the status quo and hints at future realities. Within Afrofuturism, assumptions about imperialism, postcolonialism, globalization, identity, and culture can be interrogated. With these issues in mind, I reached out to John Jennings to explore the inspiration and meaning behind Black Kirby.

Julian Chambliss: Your work has been described as Afrofuturist. What do you think of that label?
John Jennings: Even though I sometimes have issues with the prefix *Afro*futurism, I embrace that label. I think it positions the work in a historical context and also keys into a collection of themes that artists who work in this vein seem to be attracted to.

JC: In some circles, Afrofuturism is seen as resonating with the African American experience as either outsiders or exemplars in the white mainstream. Afrofuturism, they argue, lets African Americans (and others) make sense of the world. What are you trying to make sense of with Black Kirby?
JJ: I wonder if it's more in line with "creating" a new world instead of making sense of this one. I think we, as black people, have a pretty decent grasp of reality. What we are just now getting to understand is that we need a space of play, speculation, and imagination. I think that's where the notion of a space of agency exists is vital. Sun Ra was very concerned with other realities. You can see that from his film and album called *Space Is the Place*. He was dreaming of a future/fantasy space of freedom. So I think that these notions of a realm where black folk have a place is something that the Afrofuturistic or Black Speculative project is engaged with. I also feel that Afrofuturism is engaged

with a "pan-technological" viewpoint. It sees everything as a type of technology that can be hacked into, decoded, and made to function for new agenda. This includes race, religion, gender, etcetera.

JC: Traditionally, I think Afrofuturism is assumed to open a door to new ways of thinking and seeing that liberates racial minorities to "be (fill in the blank)." Black Kirby seems to blur this idea by fusing old and new. Is this a deliberate rethinking of Afrofuturism?
JJ: "Liminal." Usually people who are minorities are stereotyped and forced to live inside of that tiny little box of identity. Then, historically, public policies have been put into place to police that box. The speculative space allows minorities to imagine another self that is in another space and by doing so provides a release from that box. I think that Afrofuturism has always been about the idea of "sankofa," reaching back and getting the past and bringing it forward. The very idea of that is magical or sci-fi. So, it's not necessarily a rethinking, in my opinion. It's an uncovering of ancient ways of moving through the world but filtered through the metaphors of speculative thinking. Black Kirby is just the scion of a fusion of different creative practices that we have been undertaking for generations.

JC: Clearly Black Kirby is linked to the US superhero genre through Jack Kirby. Yet, we know questions about lack of diversity in superhero comics loom large. Are you hoping to inspire superhero comic fans and creators with Black Kirby?
JJ: Black Kirby is both a celebration of the superhero genre and also a critique. It is basically signifying on the name of Jack Kirby as a jumping-off point to discuss the lack of diversity in the superhero genre, deal with making historical connections, and investigate new ways of making meaning by fusing various modes of production found in numerous pop culture artifacts. Black Kirby is just as much hip hop as it is comics' culture, sci-fi, or postmodern.

JC: Some of your statements about Black Kirby have reference creator's rights. I think of this having powerful intersections with the black experience. Am I reading too much into your work, or do you see Black Kirby resonating with this issue?
JJ: Creator's rights is definitely something that we (Stacey and myself) are concerned with. We are both advocates for free expression in the medium and are both seasoned independent publishers. Jack Kirby's contributions to our culture is immeasurable. We felt insulted that Disney wouldn't see fit to share their bountiful profits with his family. It's just another example of how

Third Eye, from *Pitch Black Rainbow: The Art of John Jennings* (2014). © 2019 John Jennings, permission of John Jennings.

capitalism, as a religion, reshapes all aspects of morality when it comes to valuing what is actually important in our society.

JC: Black Kirby acknowledges some of the symbolic parallels inherent in Kirby's original work (Magneto as Malcolm X and Martin Luther King as Professor X) while at the same time some of the images use iconic figures from black history in Kirby's fantastic world. Can you talk about your thinking in reflecting, refracting, or refuting these parallels?

JJ: That symbolism was a retcon. It wasn't that apparent in the original stories that Kirby and [Stan] Lee did. Magneto was just another would-be ruler. The fact that he was a Jewish concentration camp survivor was added much later in the character's background. It's that idea of representation and re-presentation that Black Kirby is concerned with. Again, we are using that creative space as a way to critique the narrative and make some of those connections more apparent between the Jewish American story and the black American story. Black Kirby deals with how both peoples have used the comic's page as a space of survival and resistance.

“But They’re Ours”: John Jennings Talks about Black Superheroes

NOAH BERLATSKY / 2015

From *The Hooded Utilitarian*, June 8, 2015. https://www.hoodedutilitarian.com/2015/06/but-theyre-ours-john-jennings-talks-about-black-superheroes/. Reprinted by permission of Noah Berlatsky.

John Jennings seems like he’s got superpowers himself, he’s involved in so many projects. He teaches at the University of Buffalo. He’s involved as a curator of the Black Comix Arts Festival. He collaborates with Stacey Robinson on the Black Kirby project, he’s just coedited a new book about black identity in comics called *The Blacker the Ink*, and he’s got about a bazillion other comics projects he’s working on. And as if that’s enough, he took time out to talk to me about black superheroes, Jack Kirby, Blade, Power Man, and Captain America’s black sidekick (not that one). Our conversation is below—part of HU’s ongoing roundtable on the question of Can There Be a Black Superhero?

Noah Berlatsky: What do you like about [Jack] Kirby, and what are you less fond of?
John Jennings: I think it’s more liking than disliking. I remember being a kid and not being attracted to the work at all. I felt like he was destroying the characters that I love so much. Because his work on Captain America, as a kid, it looked blocky and crazy-looking and abstract. But for some reason you notice the work, and you’re attracted to it. And as I got older I started to realize this guy was actually creating some of the conventions, as far as how superhero comics are done. And then when we started working on the Black Kirby project, we started to realize how experimental it was. I remember reading this interview about the Black Panther. And he said he felt like his friends who were black should have a black superhero. And he did create a character who was

African and not African American. Instead of creating a black character that would be from his own country. And also the fact that Wakanda doesn't actually exist. I thought Don McGregor's run on Black Panther was in some ways really progressive. And then we turn back to Kirby, and it becomes this weird cosmic odyssey thing with this monocle dwarf guy. It's really strange. It's this odd thing to happen after a story grounded in progressive ideals because McGregor had him fighting the Klan and he was in Africa helping out his people, which was great. But I think Don McGregor as a writer has always been a lot more connected to the ideas of the black subject. You look at something like *Sabre* [graphic novel, 1978]. *Sabre* was centered in a postapocalyptic world, and the main character was an African American man. And he was in an interracial relationship with a beautiful white woman. Most of it was about him trying to protect his family. It's interesting because the character—he looked like he was loosely based on Jimi Hendrix. He was very swash-buckling, always musket and sword in hand. Had this pirate feel to it. It was a funky book, and this was Don McGregor.

NB: Yeah, I've been trying to read his *Power Man*, which I feel like he's much more conscious of racial issues. He has a hooded Klan-like supervillain attacking a black family who's trying to move into the suburbs. The writing's just hard to get through. It's not written very well.
JJ: Right—as far as—that era. If you reread the *Essential Power Man*, it's bad.

NB: It's overwritten, and it doesn't make any sense. And the dialogue's a mess.
JJ: Have you seen Jonathan Gayles's documentary *White Script, Black Supermen*? Gayles is a cultural anthropologist. The impetus for him creating the documentary was this one story where Luke Cage tries to get $200 from Doctor Doom. And he was totally disgusted by the fact that this guy was just a hustler. And that was part of the dissonance. You have a black reader, and this is the first African [American] superhero to have his own book. He is also an ex-con. And he is not necessarily really a superhero; he's a mercenary. And he's working in the hood primarily, and his villains aren't really well thought out. They didn't really understand what they were talking about with that particular character. Race in superhero comics was really strangely handled early on. Because it was directly related to blaxploitation films. Superhero comics are very reactive, they are a business, they see trends, and they try to jump on top of them. And that's pretty much what happened. That's where you get characters like Shang-Chi, who was pretty much Bruce Lee.

NB: So I'm wondering, given the inauspicious start with black superheroes, why are black superheroes important? Or why do you still care about them?
JJ: It's interesting because the superhero as a structure, it's an old idea from the 1930s. I think it's important for people who participate in society to see themselves as a hero of some kind or to see themselves in a space where they feel that they can connect with popular culture, because popular culture is our culture. That's a lot of times. The first time you see or recognize yourself is through the popular media you watch. I know it affected me as a kid coming up, watching pulp fantasy stuff and reading these things. And honestly, there's a lot of serious issues with superheroes as a genre. It's hyperviolent, it's misogynist, it's just very sexist, and it's kind of homophobic. But it's ours; it's our thing. It's an American construction. And I understand why it exists—and it does mean something when you're not there. I think that's the thing; there needs to be representation, as far as a diverse array of representations, and written from the right standpoint as well. And honestly, I think it's more important to have black creators working than it is to have black superheroes. Because there's a handful of black writers in the mainstream. One of the most important books—I don't know if it's going to get canceled—but the new *Ghost Rider* book. A Latino character, a Latino superhero, written and drawn by two African American men. That was unprecedented; I don't think people really knew that that was happening. And it's Marvel [Comics]. I think there's something about just how dominant the superhero is right now. As I think, it really is as popular as it was in the thirties. It's just not in the comics. One of the things that bothers me is that people say what kicked off the trend was the *X-Men* movies. But it was in actuality the *Blade* film. It was 1999, and that predates the *X-Men* movie.

NB: How was the *Blade* film? I haven't seen that.
JJ: *Blade* is awesome. You know why I like *Blade*? Because it's a blaxploitation movie with vampires.

NB: That sounds pretty good!
JJ: It's a fun movie. I don't know how much of this is legend and how much is truth, but Wesley Snipes, he wanted to be Black Panther. But they wouldn't let him do Black Panther, so he was like, "What else do you got?" So they gave him a c-level character. No one knew who Blade was. I knew who Blade was because I used to read the reprints, but he was kind of a lame character. He had these green goggles; it was a dumb character. But he translates really well to the screen. He's pretty much a martial artist, and Wesley Snipes is an

amazing martial artist. He's a fifth-degree black-belt. So he choreographed the entire movie. It looks great. It's out of control crazy. My friend Sundiata Cha Jua, a historian, says that after *Blade* was successful, Marvel [Studios] began to take over the franchise. When you watch the first film, it's a very "black" movie. He relies on this serum to prevent him from becoming fully a vampire; he's a daywalker. And if you look at the first movie, he gets his serum from this Afrocentric incense store. And he's in a community of black people, and they know who he is. And I thought that was really important. But when it starts making more money—because *Blade* made a lot of money—they start to dilute his connection to the black community. And they start erasing him from his own movies. As I recall, I think Wesley Snipes took them to court over the third movie because he's barely in it. It's Ryan Reynolds and Jessica Biel because they were trying to create a spin-off to Midnight Suns or something like that. Or you look at Stan Lee's movie, his documentary, which I enjoyed. But again they don't mention *Blade* as the jump off for the Marvel scene or for the Marvel franchise. Stan Lee did not create Blade. Gene Colan and Marv Wolfman created Blade. So it doesn't make sense for him to be in Stan Lee's movie. But it's false to say that the X-Men jumped off this franchise. I saw a couple of articles, like, "Hey, don't forget about the *Blade* movie."

NB: Is part of the problem with getting more black characters and more black creators is that the superheroes are so centralized in Marvel and DC? There's so much energy and interest in the big two that the only way to get a black superhero is to make Captain America black or something like that.
JJ: I have to back up a little. I'm interested in the mainstream characters. As an exercise, I think Black Kirby works because it's making fun of the superhero genre and bringing in black power politics. It's celebrating Kirby but also critiquing him. And it's interesting as a visual exercise or as a critical design project. But honestly, I don't have that much interest in mainstream superhero comics as far as black expression. I'm really not satisfied with what I've been seeing. Or the characters who I really like, they screw them up, or they do something wrong with them. Like, Mr. Terrific, I love Mr. Terrific, but his book was awful. I think the more interesting things around diversity are happening in the independent black comics' scene because it's not just superheroes. It's all these different types of genres; there's action adventure, like *Blackjack*. There's stuff like *Rigamo*, which is magical realism–gothic fantasy. So with mainstream comics there's issues around nostalgia. Nostalgia is a very powerful thing, so not only do they want to be accepted by the mainstream, they want to make a monthly comic book. It's very difficult to do that when you're

flipping burgers or you're teaching a class here or there trying to make ends meet. It's a very different model. I want to tell them, "No, make books about your experience, and put them out when you can because you're not DC." It seems like there's a problem with nostalgia and superheroes for black people since black experience in the past was often one of oppression. In the 1930s when the superheroes were created, the first black characters were extremely racist. You had characters like Whitewash, who was Captain America's sidekick and his superpower was that he always got captured and had to get rescued. He was in blackface, and he had on a zoot suit. And, of course, guys like Ebony White from *The Spirit*—they're based off how the black image had been constructed in minstrelsy and other racist propaganda. Even advertisements and products that were being generated had these extremely derogatory, hyperbolic stereotypes. So illustrators when they draw the pantomime of a black image, they're drawing from *The Jazz Singer* directly.

NB: I'm curious about what you think about the fact that one of the things for the superheroes is it's about law and order.
JJ: I think it's about justice. That's the thing—my favorite superhero is Daredevil. I totally related to this kid because I was bullied and I was poor. And I thought I was smart—I was pretty smart. I just related to that character, he was a fighter, and I liked that about the character. More than anything, I just loved the fact that he was too stupid to quit. I loved that. That's his real superpower, and that's an interesting life lesson to pick up. Don't give up. I've seen many stories where Daredevil would have died if he just gave up. But he couldn't because his father taught him not to. I thought that was awesome. Yeah, there's this thing about law and order, but they're vigilantes. And they're saying, in this resounding voice, I have the power to make things right. A lot of people were really upset when they saw Captain America punching Hitler in the face back in the day. They're violent characters. And they're reifications of a particular type of jingoistic urge. But they're ours, and they love them. I love superheroes. And I hate superheroes at the same time. I think that most folks who don't understand how these problems in our society actually manifest think that if I do this one thing then the problem is fixed. It's a very Western way of thinking. We are taught to think about the object and not the system. So making one African superhero is awesome, but what about the systemic issues around the disparity in the first place? It's the same problem with integration in our country historically. Our country would put minorities in a white space to prove a point or to illustrate a law. It hardly ever thinks once they are in this space, have we really provided a place where they can grow

Major Sankofa, from *Pitch Black Rainbow: The Art of John Jennings* (2014). © 2019 John Jennings, permission from John Jennings.

and flourish? It needs to have this token example to say, "Yeah. It's messed up in our country, but look at this ______________. See? We got that issue covered." So now we have a black writer (David Walker) on a black superhero at DC (Cyborg). Let's see how it pans out. David's a good friend and great writer. Should be exciting!

Diversifying Comics with John Jennings

GREG ANDERSON ELYSEE / 2015

From TheOutsiders.Com, August 24, 2015. http://www.theouthousers.com/index.php/columns/132982-diversifying-with-john-jennings-griot-vine-interview.html. Reprinted by permission of Greg Anderson Elysee.

Greg Anderson Elysee: Welcome to (Heard it Thru) The Griot Vine, Mr. John Jennings! It's an honor to have you here!
John Jennings: I am honored to be here. Thanks for the interest in my work!

GAE: Are you kidding me? You're amazing! How are you today?
JJ: I am doing just fine.

GAE: There are many people living under a rock. Can you please educate them and tell us about yourself?
JJ: Let's see. Again, my name is John Jennings. I am an associate professor of art and visual studies at the University at Buffalo State University of New York (SUNY). I teach in the graphic design program. I study stereotypes in popular media concerning the constructions of black identity. In particular, I look at science fiction, fantasy, comics, and other types of cartoons and caricatures that depict blackness and its mediations. I am also an illustrator, author, curator, and comics' artist. I am a freelance graphic designer, and I have designed a lot of notable covers around Afrofuturism, including the Afrofuturism book by Ytasha Womack, *Octavia's Brood* edited by Adrienne Maree Brown and Walidah Amarisha, and *Mothership* edited by Bill Campbell and Ed Hall. I also designed the Samuel R. Delany Tribute Collection Stories for Chip book cover published by Rosarium Publishing, edited by Bill Campbell and Nisi Shawl. I am the coauthor of several books on race and identity in comics, including *The Blacker the Ink* with Frances Gateward and *Black Comix* with Damian Duffy. I am also the cofounder and coorganizer of the Black Comic Book Festival in Harlem, New

York, at the historic Schomburg Center for Research in Black Culture and MLK/NORCAL's Black Comix Arts Festival in San Francisco. My next major project is the graphic novel adaptation of Octavia Butler's classic novel *Kindred* along with my long-time collaborator and good friend Damian Duffy.

GAE: How long have you been into comics, as a reader and creator? How did you get involved in it?
JJ: I have been into comics since I was a child. I was always an active and avid reader from the jump. I'd read a lot of tall tales, myths, and legends from all over the world. One day, my mother bought me *The Mighty Thor* and the *Amazing Spider-Man*, and I was pretty much hooked. I must have been, like, nine years old, maybe? I started drawing around the age of four, and I have always been fascinated by images. I got really serious about comics again when I was going for tenure at the University of Illinois at Urbana-Champaign. So the early 2000s? Since then, I have been doing shows, events, and creation around diversity in comics.

GAE: So what is going on with *Kindred*? Can you tell us about it? I'm excited for this book because the novel is one of my absolute favorites.
JJ: The *Kindred* graphic novel was stalled a bit on the publisher's side due to a change in personnel. Damian and I are now full steam ahead on the production of the book. I have taken a research leave to devote my time to the book. ABRAMS ComicArts plans to release it in 2017. So right now we are in a flurry to get it done and out! Thanks for the patience.

GAE: *Kindred* is a pretty heavy book. For the people unfamiliar with it, can you tell us what it's about?
JJ: *Kindred* is a dark fantasy book that was written in the mid-seventies by the amazing Octavia Butler that details the adventures of an interracial couple's (black woman and white man) supernatural travels back into time from 1976 to a Maryland slave plantation. The book deals with the trauma related to chattel slavery and the intricate relationships that occurred in that horrible time in our nation's history and how those relationships still connect to us to this very day.

GAE: What are you bringing to this adaptation? And what has the creative process been like? Are there a lot of reworked scenes?
JJ: I think the main part that is being added is the visual, honestly. We have tried to be as honest with the adaptation as humanly possible, letting Octavia's

voice take the lead. So there have been very little additions to the original story. As you said, some people have never read the book, so it would be a disservice to them to not just introduce the book as is.

GAE: You brought up your longtime collaborator, Damian Duffy, and you two have worked together for quite some time! How did you first meet, and how did this creative union start?
JJ: Our creative process is very fluid. Damian and I have been working together on various projects for a decade. We met at the University at Illinois at Urbana-Champaign when I was teaching there. Damian is a PhD student currently in the Library Information Sciences Department. When I was there I managed to bring Scott McCloud to the campus. Damian attended and through a system of coincidences ended up having dinner with us. We met up again at a talk I was doing and ended up becoming friends and collaborators. Our process is very open and give-and-take. Damian is a very talented writer and editor. I think that we bring out the best in each other creatively. That's why we've tolerated each other for ten years! [Laughs]

GAE: I'm originally familiar with *The Hole: Consumer Culture [Volume One]*, a work both you and Damian created.
JJ: *The Hole: Consumer Culture* was our response to Hurricane Katrina and the total mishandling of that tragedy. It focused on the demonization of the black body and the subsequent buying and selling of race in America. It's also, as you said of *Kindred*, a heavy book. We are used to dealing with difficult subjects in the work.

GAE: An aspect that I loved with *The Hole* was the focus on the bastardization of black spirituality. The Vodou spirituality plays a pretty big part of the story, especially in how Hollywood has converted black spirituality into a form of horror storytelling and evil, and goes into the complexity of a character like Papa Legba. What brought about the decision to dwell on these themes? I'm sure this goes hand-in-hand with your interest of breaking down stereotypes within your work.
JJ: So a lot of people don't realize this, but *The Hole* was originally a white character that I did as a graphic novel by myself. I am kind of ashamed of it now, but it was the first time I stretched out as a comic creator. A lot of the themes actually came from there. That narrative took its supernatural aspect from the Judeo-Christian-Gnostic idea of the sin-eater. Since we were being inspired by Katrina, we decided to do research on Vodou. A great deal

of practitioners live in New Orleans. We took a cue from that fact. The book became something totally different then. Sometimes it felt as it if it wrote itself. It was critically acclaimed and has been taught at major universities across the world. So I guess we did something right? A large part of *The Hole* was definitely geared towards unpacking stereotypes. *The Hole* has a teaching guide in the back, a bibliography, and a glossary of terms. We made it to be taught.

GAE: So you find yourself cringing looking back at your original version of *The Hole*, like most writers and artists looking back?
JJ: I think we all look back and cringe at earlier work. There was promise in the original story, but I have come a very long way as a storyteller and artist.

GAE: Another thing that strongly stood out to me reading was the unflinching portrayal of sex. The book was pretty explicit, but I felt it added to the raw storytelling going on with the portrayal and deconstruction of the black body. Was this a conscious decision, and what prompted you and Damian to just go all out with the sexuality? People are usually prudes when it comes to this.
JJ: *The Hole* is an uncomfortable book. It was hard for us to delve into those areas at first, but the hypersexualization of the black body is a part of the narrative and it had to be dealt with. The book is made to be problematic in the right ways. We wanted this book to be taught and studied, so you have to know the space enough to "go there" and be ready to defend your choices. So sexuality in our society is treated as this taboo thing, yet violence is naturalized.

GAE: No sense at all.
JJ: It makes no sense. So we will most likely be exploring these aspects more in coming projects for sure. People have desires and are attracted to a lot of things that aren't heteronormative. That is demonized in our society. So dealing with a shape-shifting hyperbolic body talks about that openly. We have to make spaces for conversation . . . literally poke holes in old notions about identity and the fiction of normality.

GAE: Now you do know I'm still waiting for volume two of *The Hole*, right? I'm just saying . . . you left me hanging there. What are the plans for volume two, if any?
JJ: We are planning to eventually do *The Hole, Volume 2*. We have been talking about it recently . . . especially since the visit we made to Vassar College. It's down the road a bit more though. We have a ton of projects that are in front

of it . . . *unless* some publisher wants to publish it for us . . . That original book is just full of rage and anguish because of injustice. I think it'd be hard to pick up on that now . . . we are still energetic and outraged about what's been going on in society, but I think our voices have become much savvier and, honestly, more creative.

GAE: You've also been working on *Blue Hand Mojo* and *Kid Code*! You have absolutely *no* idea how much fun I had reading those books.
JJ: Thanks so much!

GAE: Can you tell us about the creative process?
JJ: Well, *Blue Hand Mojo* is something that's been in my head for a while . . . maybe four or five years? I've stopped and started on it several times. I ended up plotting out a complete story and then decided that before I do that story . . . I needed to spend more time in that creative world so that audiences knew what I was doing. Stories have to have room to breathe sometimes. That takes time. So I ended up coming up with three shorter stories that I am now working on to collect as a trade. I plan to do another collection like that . . . *then* do the longer graphic novel. Also, I have some other plans to collaborate with others on that character. I have some really cool plans for Half-Dead Johnson! [Laughs]

GAE: I'm excited!
JJ: *Kid Code* was a blast to work on with Stacey [Robinson] and Damian. It was truly a hip-hop comic. So Stacey and I planned out the initial world and story. Then I used dice to literally use freestyle and chance to decide how many panels would be on a page.

GAE: Dice?! Wait . . . so you literally rolled dice to plot your pages? How the heck?
JJ: Yep. I basically gave myself a high and low number of dots to hit and threw dice to let chance decide what would happen on each page. Then I created a visual script that told Stacey exactly what size panels to use . . . POV, etcetera. It was a great way to write. He would edit panels as he needed, and Damian could just focus on the dialogue and the lettering. I wrote a very insane story, and Damian totally edited and remixed it, made it better. Stacey did the pencils for *Kid Code*. I did inks and colors. Then Damian lettered and wrote over the images. It was a mash-up of epic proportions! We are working on number two of a three-part arc. Can't wait!

GAE: How long did *Kid Code* take from initial conception? One of my favorite things about the book was how surreal it was. It was a little confusing. But when I read through it a second time, I took it in more, and everything just clicked. It made it such an amazing experience. Was that intentional, or did you just get lucky?
JJ: *Kid Code* took about four months or so? The initial conception started out from a long drive from Buffalo to Columbus. Stacey and I were going to speak at a comic forum at the Columbus College of the Arts, and I pitched him this idea about a time-traveling superhero who was inspired by hip hop. We riffed from there and built this wild story! Damian brought in the finishing touches . . . his dialogue and humor was just perfect for the story. It's obviously very similar in some ways to *The Hole* in that it's an anticapitalist narrative. It's packed with a lot of information. Our work tends to have multiple layers. This was very collaborative and freestyled, but I think we knew we had a special mix from the start. Looking forward to working in that world more.

GAE: Dude, where the heck do you have the time to do everything? You're a bit of a jack-of-all-trades with art and writing, you teach, and you got married about a year ago, right? How do you manage? Do you have clones because I feel like each week I learn you're working on something else?
JJ: How do you eat a whale?

GAE: With tartar sauce, maybe? Like a *ton*.
JJ: [Laughs] Even with tartar sauce, you have to eat it a little at a time. People want an app for success, and there just isn't. A lot of these things take a lot of planning and collaboration over many years. For instance, that *The Blacker the Ink* collection that I coedited with Frances Gateward, that took, like, five years to finish. You work a bit here . . . a bit there. Before you know it . . . you have a lot of work. A comic is done one line at a time. One panel at a time. One page at a time. It's not a race. It's a marathon. People ask me all the time how much I sleep or how I manage. I think that most people aren't happy or fulfilled with what they do. Some people downright hate what they do for a living. I love what I do. It's difficult work. It's arduous . . . but I love it, so it's not work to me.

GAE: So what is your creative process like?
JJ: My creative process is methodical. I do a lot of research on things. I read broadly and deeply. I have a personal library that I consult on the regular and add to when needed. I make a lot of sketches and scribbles. I edit down a lot. My writing process and my art-making process are both informed by my

training as a designer. That's another mindset that helps you work on many things. As a freelancer, if you don't have a bunch of things going, you starve. Also you learn that from the academy—publish or perish. If you are at a university and you don't get tenure, that's it. You are out of a gig. So you have to keep pushing, and I think that it just becomes part of you. Another thing: I don't have kids. . . yet! [Laughs]

GAE: Yet. [Laughs] I wonder if your wife, Tawana, is reading . . .
JJ: Oh, believe me. She is . . .

GAE: Haha. What inspires you to keep on going?
JJ: My main inspiration is that I want to, in some way, leave the world better than when I got here. I am also very dedicated to helping alternative voices be heard. Also, death keeps me going. Our time on this earth is short. I want to make the most of time on this plane of existence. I know that sounds morbid, but it makes me appreciate what I have and what I can offer.

GAE: The very first work from you I discovered was actually the David Banner series you did animation for called *Walking with Gods*. How did you get involved in that?
JJ: David got wind of the Black Kirby project from a longtime friend who saw the show at Jackson State. David called me one morning, and we talked about what he needed. It was a great project to work on!

GAE: Do you know if Banner thought of expanding further and getting you involved?
JJ: I know that David is focusing on his commitments as an activist at the moment. He also has a new album about to drop called *The God Box* that deals with a lot of the issues that are affecting our people on the ground today. *Walking with Gods* is an extension of that idea. He wanted to give our children a new hero, a symbol of hope. So you haven't seen the last of Alex Light, but I can't openly say what the next steps are.

GAE: What are your thoughts on the state of race and overall diversity within comics? What do you think is working and not working? And what could be improved?
JJ: That's the hardest question yet. I have made it my business to deal with diversity on all fronts regarding the comics industry. It's come a long way, but there is much more ground to cover. You have to come at the problem

on multiple fronts, diversity in readership, diversity in content, diversity in characters, diversity in creators, and diversity in the people who publish and distribute these books. So there are more independent books out there, and technology has allowed for us to get our work to a much, much broader audience. Just look at what Bill Campbell has done with Rosarium, what Regine Sawyer has done with Lockett Down, and what Imani Lateef has done with Peep Game Comix. There's a huge upsurge in talent, and there's a community that we have built that supports it. The mainstream is listening a bit now. There are a few really great titles that are pushing boundaries: *Bitch Planet*, *Rat Queens*, *Wolf*, *Ms. Marvel*, and the new *Cyborg* comic from DC Comics, written by *Shaft* scribe David Walker. One really cool book that hardly anyone talks about was the Latino *Ghost Rider*! It was a cool book! It wasn't *The Watchmen*, but it was a solid read. At the end of the run it was written by Felipe Smith and drawn by the dope Damion Scott. And it was about a *Latino* kid taking care of his disabled brother. Two black creators on a book with a Latino lead at *Marvel Comics*? Unheard of! No one talks about it though. Oh by the way, I'd be remiss to mention the lackluster Falcon as *Captain America* book and the even more uneven *Storm* solo series. How is it that these characters have been around for decades and they don't know who they are? But as I understand, there are also new books on the horizon and the new Milestone Media getting ready to push out more work soon! The main issue is that the largest comic book publishers aren't comic book publishers. They are multinational conglomerates disguised as comics companies. They really don't care about true diversity overall and don't really care about the audiences. If they did, they would change how they operate. They only care about the bottom line, and this mythical notion that everyone wants the stuff they are putting out. When in actuality they would reach more people by just changing a few things. However, DC and Marvel in particular are institutions. Institutions *suck* at changing. That's ok. *We* will change it.

GAE: I'm determined to be a part of that change! You've hit on a lot of points there but what of the audience?
JJ: The mainstream comics' audience is nerdish-ly devoted to the superhero genre, and this perpetuates the notion that comics are only good for doing superhero-driven narratives. It's this horrible vicious cycle like something out of the third act of that Ang Lee *Hulk* film!

GAE: Ouch . . .

JJ: Another horrible thing is that folks who are creators and happen to be white men are looking through privileged lenses . . . and don't realize it. So you have a Mark Waid, who writes a story that is supposed to deal with racism in Mississippi in the 1920s but ends up composing a hackneyed collection of stereotypes via a white male perspective. Then you have an Ales Kot, who creates a new book (*Wolf*) with a black protagonist and after the fifth issue plans to feature creators of color in the back of the book. He has also turned down writing jobs at Marvel that he felt would be better written by someone other than a white straight male author. So you see two totally different paradigms there. These are happening in the industry *right now*. The last thing is distribution . . . (sigh)

GAE: As an indie creator working to break in, I'll add a sigh right there with you. (sigh)
JJ: (sigh) We have a monopoly in charge of what books get distributed to comic retailers. Diamond distribution has some very weird and, honestly, unfair policies when dealing with independent books. However, there are alternative spaces . . . and we have to go there and figure out ways to open up the market. There's an audience yearning to hear our stories, and we can't let a handful of privileged folk control our destiny. America doesn't work that way.

GAE: Sadly, when it comes to quite a large number of consumers of color, the only time diversity really matters to them is if it's from DC or Marvel. It's such an uphill battle.
JJ: A main issue around the buzzword of diversity is that it's only important when large multinational companies do it. The Black Age of Comics Movement has been around for over twenty years now, and it's still a relatively unknown counterculture. It's a hot topic now for them, but it's been the life's work of so many of our colleagues. Marvel makes Thor a woman and Captain America black, and it's the best thing that ever happened since *Understanding Comics* was published. The BBC interviewed me at length last year regarding diversity in comics. I focused on the black indie side of things. None of my interview was used. A black female reporter from a large network approached me about a story regarding diversity in comics and again . . . I spoke about the independent work, the events, and the awards that are happening yet getting no fanfare. We spoke for about two hours. I also told her to some effect, "I know you can't really use any of this because we aren't Disney or Viacom . . . but I wanted you to know, sister." Nothing came of it. "Diversity" writ large . . . is

just a box someone checks on a form in some cold office space. However, this . . . this work is what we do. When the cameras are gone and the networks stop caring, me and my sisters and brothers will still be here . . . Sometimes alone in front of a table or computer, ruining our posture and eyes . . . panel by panel, building something that looks like a future we need to see.

GAE: I feel like most consumers who want to find books of diversity, and creators also, have that breaking point where they say, "That's it. I'm done with this. I need to find something else that reflects me and others." What was that moment for you?
JJ: I think the turning point was in 2005 when the Masters of American Comics art show was touring, and there weren't any women in it. That was a wake-up call for me. There are gatekeepers, and you can't play with us. It's a type of violence. People don't think of it that way, but it kills your spirit to not see yourself reflected in society.

GAE: What has been some of your biggest challenges being a black creator in the industry?
JJ: I think being black has been a challenge! [Laughs]

GAE: Ha!
JJ: Seriously though, you have to realize that most of my career has been as an academic. I have fought the battles around diversity in the classroom and in the academy for over seventeen years now. I am a relative new voice to anything that resembles the mainstream. So I'd say I've had the same challenges, but when you add race to equation, it does become much more difficult, whether people want to acknowledge that or not.

GAE: What has been some of the most rewarding?
JJ: The most rewarding aspects of my career have been the creation of new spaces, publications, and events where people can feel empowered, safe, and connected to others that make and feel as they do. When you don't see yourself reflected in the world, it causes a type of trauma. I think that I've had some hand in making experiences and spaces of healing. That feels great.

GAE: You're one of the show runners of the Black Comic Fest. Thank you for that! That has been one of my favorite events of the year. What was the initial thought process starting it, and what has the journey been like? How has it grown? And where would you like to take it?

JJ: The Black Comic Book Festival in Harlem is one of my proudest achievements. Deirdre Hollman, Jonathan Gayles, Jerry Craft, and I founded it, and it was basically a meeting of the minds. We found that we all had common goals and decided to come together. It was kind of serendipity. The process was pretty rocky at first because you have two cultures coming together to figure out how to work together properly. Once we got past that we realized that we all wanted the same thing: for our people to celebrate their creativity and to fuel the imagination of our young ones. The first one brought in over thirteen hundred people. The event has now more than doubled in size. So we want it to continue growing and inspiring. As of now it's part of a network of these events that hopefully can provide an alternative space for these creators to shine. Last year I cofounded with Aaron Grizzell, Collete Rodgers-Grizzell, Ayize Jama Everett, David Walker, and Shawn Taylor the Black Comix Arts Festival in San Francisco. It was a big success as well and hopefully will grow like the Schomburg event. It takes place on MLK day, the same weekend as the New York event. So MLK Weekend is now a coast-to-coast celebration of black indie comics! It's wonderful. In October, I am colaunching with Dr. Frederick Aldama and Ricardo Padilla (founder of the Latino Comics Expo) a new event called SOL-CON: The Brown and Black Comix Expo. It's a historic teaming of Latino and black indie comics' creators on the campus of the Ohio State University. It's going to be in tandem with a new comics' festival there called CXC. It's going to be fabulous!

GAE: What advice, tips, or warnings can you give creators, writers, and artists trying to get into comics?
JJ: My advice is don't try to get into comics. Just make comics . . . and create honestly with your own voice. Time is short. Don't let anyone stop you from telling your stories. There's no reason to not make what you feel you need to make.

GAE: What else is currently on your platter?
JJ: My platter? (sigh) I honestly can't list it all. I am cocurating a show right now called *Unveiling Visions: The Alchemy of the Black Imagination* with Dr. Reynaldo Anderson. The show will be open to the public on the twenty-fifth of September and run through late December. My friend and collaborator Stacey Robinson is our art director on that event. So exciting! Lot of work, but so exciting! My new book that I coedited with Dr. Frances Gateward just dropped in summer. It's a collection of fifteen essays by top scholars regarding the portrayal of black identity in comics; it's called *The Blacker the Ink*. You can find

Conjurer and root-worker Frank "Half-Man Johnson," from *Pitch Black Rainbow: The Art of John Jennings* (2014). © 2019 John Jennings, permission of John Jennings.

my own art book available as well: *Pitch Black Rainbow*. As I stated before I am working on *Blue Hand Mojo* and *Kid Code* (with Damian Duffy and Stacey Robinson of Black Kirby). But my two biggest projects are Octavia Butler's *Kindred*, the graphic novel adaptation with Damian Duffy, and *The Bluesman* with my friend Stuart Jaffe. Imagine the Ralph Macchio film *Crossroads* mixed with the TV show *Supernatural* with a touch of a samurai story. I am also working on a graphic novel with Nalo Hopkinson called *Nancy Jack* and a graphic novel with Ayize Jama Everett called *Box of Bones* along with a team of talented pencillers. It's like "Afrocentric Hellraiser," a ten part story that takes place throughout the diaspora. Oh! And I am coediting *APB: Artists against Police Brutality* with Bill Campbell and Jason Rodriguez for Rosarium Publishing. I could go on, but it would make me cry . . .

GAE: You did it to yourself. I told you, you're a mad man. Where can we find and stalk you?
JJ: You can stalk me on twitter at: Twitter: @JIJennings. Tumblr: http://jijennin70.tumblr.com/.

GAE: John Jennings, ladies and gents!

Black Art: Why the Artistic Commentary of John Jennings Is So Important

SHEENA C. HOWARD / 2015

From HuffPost.Com, December 30, 2015. https://www.huffpost.com/entry/post_b_8892290. Reprinted by permission of Sheena C. Howard.

As a diversity of voices sounds anew to effect change—and as movements coalesce around related causes—it's worth remembering one essential from the realm of artistic commentary: Black cartoonists need to be a prominent part of our ongoing national conversation, says Michael Cavna of the *Washington Post*. There is one artistic voice that stands out above the rest as pivotal to the national conversation around race, identity, and social justice. That is the voice of John Jennings, visual artist pioneer and author. The artistic work of John Jennings should not escape any contemporary conversation on black visual artists of the twenty-first century. John Jennings, cocurator of Unveil*ing Visions: The Alchemy of the Black Imagination*, offers a fresh perspective on black imagination and challenges our notions of black expression in popular culture by forcing those that engage with his work to envision a future that inverts our notion of the historical and contemporary black experience. John Jennings visual work offers up hope at a time when much of the black community feels despair and plight as we powerlessly, yet consciously live with the daily forces of physical and mental brutality upon our bruised bodies. Within a system that fails to provide security, protection, and justice for black folks, the visual work of John Jennings often portrays a world in which black people have control over their bodies, live outside the confines of rigid boxes, and shatter the struggle of policed expression.

John Jennings visual work needs to be a part of the national conversation on race, identity, and social justice. Here's why:

1. Social movements always coalesce around symbols that act as unifying motifs to empower and embolden an oppressed group of people. In 2015, John Jennings created a remix of the black Twitter icon, which instantly went viral on Twitter using #BLKPWRTWITTR. The significance of this icon cannot go understated. For Jennings the icon was a visual response to the murders of nine innocent black Americans in the historic Mother Emanuel AME Church in Charleston, South Carolina. Users all across Twitter and Facebook changed their profile pictures to the black Twitter logo created by Jennings. Jennings says, "I decided to make something to deal with how I was feeling but also to show unity via a symbol. Ironically, I am not a huge user of Twitter. I do know, however, that Twitter has been used to organize, spread information, and do critical analyses of current events by black scholars and activists regarding the community. I wanted to make something that represented that. So I amalgamated the Twitter symbol with the classic notion of Black Power."

2. Jennings work aesthetically challenges our notions of black masculinity and femininity, challenges stereotypes of African Americans, and produces visual commentary that is politically charged. Jennings says, "We have to understand that stereotypical images are designed to function in a particular way. They all have purposes in how the black body is perceived. The work that I do and that my colleagues create offer alternatives to those constructions and gives the black audience choices on multiple levels." This is an important artistic motivation on two levels. First, his work allows us to break out of the rigid boxes of identity that have been inscribed upon black people. Second, this is particularly important as we consider the labeling of black bodies as deviant in which the state then uses this logic to justify police brutality and lethal force, even when it comes to black children. His work offers up hope, even if just momentarily, that the black body is more than the historical prescribed labels that allow for society to control and devalue blacks in destructive ways.

3. The mixture and history of John Jennings's work is the site of contemporary black visual art harboring an amalgamation of intellectual critique juxtaposed with the imagination of a new black cultural identity. Jennings's work does not shy away from a future that sees the black community as conquering sexism, racism, and heterosexism. John Jennings's work does not reinforce a future that views women as devalued or LGBTQ people as deviant (see the cover art for *Black Queer Identity Matrix*). Instead his work exhibits hope for a future in which oppression of any kind across the black community is destroyed. Jennings says, "As a cultural activist and creator, I try to create

The Shadow Knows, from *Pitch Black Rainbow: The Art of John Jennings* (2014).
© 2019 John Jennings, permission of John Jennings.

stories and characters that are truly subjective and flexible and have myriad representations and modes of existence."

4. Across the academic landscape, Jennings's book cover art is untouchable. Jennings is the creative brains and designer of numerous notable books including, but not limited to, Dr. James Peterson's *The HipHop Underground and African American Culture*; the Eisner Award–winning book *Black Comics Politics of Race and Representation*, and Ytasha L. Womack's *Afrofuturism: The World of Black Sci Fi and Fantasy Culture*. This is to name a few. A quick glance at Jennings's cover art will portray a notable aspect of Jennings's work, which is the varied expressions of blackness represented aesthetically, as well as the beautiful ways in which his characters look, well, black. This is important as white creators struggle to draw the cultural nuances of black features when creating black comic characters.

5. John Jennings is not only a cultural producer but also a cultural preserver with iconic works such as Black Kirby. Black Kirby forces us to connect our cultural past, to our present, and imagine the future within the realm of comics' history. Black Kirby also functions as a highly syncretic mytho-poetic framework by appropriating Jack Kirby's bold forms and revolutionary ideas combined with themes centered around Afrofuturism, social justice, black history, media criticism, science fiction, magical realism, and the utilization of hip-hop culture as a methodology for creating visual expression.

John Jennings's cocurated exhibit *Unveiling Visions: The Alchemy of the Black Imagination* at the Schomburg Center in Harlem, New York, has been extended to January 16, due to its popularity. According to the New York Public Library site, *Unveiling Visions: The Alchemy of the Black Imagination* includes artifacts from the Schomburg collections that are connected to Afrofuturism, black speculative imagination and diasporic cultural production. The exhibit offers a fresh perspective on the power of speculative imagination and the struggle for various freedoms of expression in popular culture.

The Soul of Black Comics: An Interview with John Jennings

JULIAN CHAMBLISS / 2017

From Black Perspectives.Com, October 14, 2017. Reprinted by permission of AAIHS.

This month I had the opportunity to speak with John Jennings, professor of media and cultural studies and a cooperating faculty member in the Department of Creative Writing at the University of California Riverside. Jennings is a scholar and artist whose artistic work is deeply influenced by the African American cultural experience and explores intersectional narratives linked to identity. He illustrated Octavia Butler's *Kindred: A Graphic Novel Adaptation*. He recently completed a stint as the Nasir Jones Hiphop Fellow at the Hutchins Center, Harvard University. While Jennings's adaptation of Butler's *Kindred* has generated excitement, his original creative work highlights a creative intervention designed to celebrate black culture. Jennings is coeditor of *The Blacker the Ink: Constructions of Black Identity in Comics and Sequential Art* and cofounder/organizer of the Schomburg Center's Black Comic Book Festival, the Black Comix Arts Festival in San Francisco, and the SOL-CON: The Brown and Black Comix Expo at the Ohio State University. I spoke with him about his latest graphic novel *Blue Hand Mojo* (Rosarium Publishing, an innovative publishing startup dedicated to bringing multicultural voices to the public). Follow Professor Jennings on Twitter @JIJennings.

Julian Chambliss: You have recently grabbed a lot of attention with your adaptation of *Kindred*. How does *Blue Hand Mojo* offer a different creative experience for you?
John Jennings: The opportunity to do *Kindred* with my long-time collaborator and friend Damian Duffy has been a remarkable experience. Octavia Butler is one of the most important American writers to ever live. However, *Blue*

Hand Mojo is totally my own creation from top to bottom. The experience of essentially collaborating with another writer is vastly different than controlling the entire narrative. With *Mojo* I could make format changes, rearrange story elements, and enhance the narrative as I worked on it. You don't have the same range of freedom when you are doing such a beloved book as *Kindred*.

JC: In *Blue Hand Mojo*, you focus on the figure Half Dead Johnson. What is it about Half Dead Johnson that you wanted to bring to life as an African American scholar, writer, and artist?
JJ: Half Dead is the fictional first cousin of the legendary blues musician Robert Johnson. I wanted to take something from our cultural history that was already a piece of folklore and then push it even further. Half Dead represents the raw anger and pain that was the burden of black men and women working under the weight of the Jim Crow South. His revenge on his white attackers and his subsequent curse to work for the devil represent the fact that those experiences followed black people with them during the various stages of the Great Migration. I wanted to explore what that does to a person but also use the supernatural as the lens through which to view the narrative implications.

JC: Your story is steeped in the cultural legacy of the African American experience, but shows a depth and complexity around race, community, and identity. What were your goals in crafting this story?
JJ: I am from Mississippi, and I carry a lot of the weight of the racism in our country in my own personal experience. It's a haunted existence sometimes. This is why I coined the term (with Stanford Carpenter) "EthnoGothic." It is dealing with very complex tensions around the black experience in the United States and in particular the black southern experience. It's also dealing with how trauma acts as a revenant of our continually contentious narratives around race, class, and history. Even as I answer these questions, protesters use their bodies to occlude a white woman's painting of Emmett Till. Our past isn't done with us. It's not even the past.

JC: You have been a consistent voice helping to create space where scholars and practitioners are in dialogue. Your work seems to model that process. How do you see this kind of creative intervention evolving in the future?
JJ: I think that I can see my practice evolving into one of producer, editor, and facilitator. I have a knack for being able to find overlaps across disciplines and between scholars from various modes of discourse. My most important

Portrait of science fiction, fantasy, African-futurism writer Nnedi Okorafor. © 2019 John Jennings, permission of John Jennings.

asset, however, isn't a skill set at all; it's a point of view that I fervently believe and constantly put into practice. I truly want us all to be successful. I truly believe that by working together we can achieve anything. So I have dedicated my career and my energies to creating opportunities where many individuals have the potential to move forward and find agency in the experience. I think that if we can make collaboration the norm and not the exception, we would be totally amazed by what we can accomplish.

JC: What is on the horizon for your creative work exploring the black experience and black identity?

JJ: I just finished up toning pages for a book with Tony Medina and Stacey Robinson called *I Am Alfonso Jones*. It's a black-and-white graphic novel from Lee and Low/Tu Books that deals with the death of a bicultural teenage boy named Alfonso Jones. The entire story is told from the boy's perspective as a ghost. The book deals with social justice, police brutality, and the Black Lives Matter Movement. I just signed a contract with Rosarium Publishing to put out a ten-part maxiseries with Ayize Jama Everett called *Box of Bones*. The story follows a black queer southern woman who is doing her dissertation fieldwork around a mysterious artifact that punishes people who have wronged people of color throughout the African diaspora. The scholar, little by little, realizes that the artifact is real and that her destiny is connected to it. It's not for the squeamish. I use the elevator pitch of "Afrocentric Hellraiser" to give the context in a quick sound bite. The terror begins this fall. Damian Duffy and I are currently finishing up *Black Comix Returns*. It's the follow up to our 2010 art book, *Black Comix: African American Independent Comic, Art, and Culture*. This book, which was fully backed on Kickstarter, will be a 12 x 12 in., hardcover, full-color art book with double the amount of independent black comics' creators inside. It should be coming your way in early spring 2018. There are more things coming, but I am not at liberty to talk about them just yet. Thanks so much for the opportunity to talk about this work.

From Dark Water to Dark Matter: An Interview with John Jennings

TIFFANY BARBER / 2018

From *Cosmic Underground: A Grimoire of Black Speculative Discontent*, 2018. Reprinted by permission of Rochon Perry of Cedar Grove Publishing.

This conversation was transcribed from a Skype conversation regarding the curation of the art exhibition *Unveiling Visions: The Alchemy of the Black Imagination*, which was featured at the Schomburg Center and cocurated by Reynaldo Anderson and John Jennings.

Tiffany Barber: Tell me about the curation-al vision for the show.
John Jennings: One of the constructions Kevin Young puts forth in *The Grey Album: On the Blackness of Blackness* is the notion of the shadow book. He defines it as this fictitious artifact, this book that haunts the existence of an existing book—for instance, the Encyclopedia Africana that W. E. B. Du Bois never finished or Ralph Ellison's second novel. So it's this book that actually should have happened, or could have happened, but didn't. And the memory of it haunts the existence of an existing book. I love that idea. I started thinking there are whole libraries of books that could be like that—Schomburg's library! So my mind went to these different spaces, and I wondered what about shadow objects and shadow worlds? That's how we came up with these diegetic prototypes that were influenced by actual things. One of them was the theoretical elevators book from Colson Whitehead's *The Intuitionist*—

TB: Oh yeah!
JJ: That's not a real book, but I created a cover for it.

TB: Right, right.

JJ: Or these objects that people have described in black speculative fiction, like the flying shoes with the propellers in Amiri Baraka's short story "Mchawi" or the chair from George Schuyler's *Black No More*. Our whole thing was creating fictitious, shadow objects in line with what these types of speculative, interventionist technologies would look like.

TB: Very cool.
JJ: One thing we didn't get a chance to do was the bop gun.

TB: The what?
JJ: The bop gun from George Clinton/Parliament Funkadelic.

TB: Ahhhh! Next time. [Laughter]
JJ: Yeah, it was on our minds.

TB: Okay, so you talked about the shadow book. But *Unveiling Visions* also draws on key concepts put forth by W. E. B. Du Bois in the first half of the twentieth century, namely double consciousness and the veil. How did these concepts give rise to yours and Reynaldo's curatorial for the show?
JJ: Yes. The title *Unveiling Visions* comes directly from the construct of the veil, from Du Bois's classic treatise on black identity, *The Souls of Black Folk*. He also talks about writing from within the veil in *Darkwater*. The veil is an extension; it's a technology. I mean, think about if the veil was an app or a prosthetic that we could peer through. We regard Du Bois's veil not as this negative apparatus that splits us and makes us see things differently, but as a superpower. How does that shift the perspective of black people, particularly in a black space like the Schomburg? In this vein, we started thinking about the Schomburg as a time capsule, looking at it as a spaceship or some other type of apparatus. So these shadow objects we're talking about—what does it mean to introduce people to these different concepts around black speculative culture that have been around forever? People who are working in these black speculative spaces are saying, "You know what? Not only have we been imagining these spaces before, we don't necessarily have to draw from a Westernized ideology as far as how we're creating these stories. We have other pillars we rely on." Take Sheree Renee Thomas's work, for example. I didn't realize until we posted the books from the show on Facebook that her primary research was conducted at the Schomburg. So it comes full circle because her ideas in that book are fundamental to what we're talking about in the show—how do you even define what is black speculative culture? Where

does it stop; where does it start? What does it mean to speculate? That kind of thing.

TB: Yeah, in the exhibition text you and Reynaldo talk about how the work in the exhibition explores not only the notion of blackness's twoness, but also how these concepts have so long been mired in a drive toward assimilation or acceptance. Most, if not all of the work in the show, points to other possibilities. What is the relationship between these historical concepts and imagining new racial futures? Can you also talk about the relationship between the past, present, and future that emerges in the show?

JJ: It's almost like this show became more powerful in the black space of the Schomburg because of how it connects the past to the present and these ideas of future stories to be told. It just felt like a great confluence of a lot of different ideas. It also started us thinking about race, which is one of the biggest speculations, right? It's a diegetic prototype that has taken hold and dovetails with a lot of what we're talking about: what is technology, how does it function, what are the blueprints for these kinds of systemic issues (like racism), and how do the images become touchstones for possible answers to these questions, i.e. possible futures? They could be right beside each other. That's actually what I think this notion of double consciousness affords us; we can think in multiple dimensions. And when you add Fanonian triple consciousness, it splinters into quantum ideas, to borrow from Rasheedah Phillips's idea of Black Quantum Futurism. So the more we explored these concepts and spaces, the more the show expanded. There are eighty-seven artists in the show, and what made that possible was the technology available to us. We used mostly digital work, prints, and virtual constructions. And we did most of the exhibition design remotely. Turns out Isissa Komada-John is a master at Sketch Up, and she built a virtual replica of the Latimer/Edison gallery using that software. I created these teeny-tiny jpegs to scale according to the model she put together and placed them along the wall of the virtual model. Another tool we used, when we were gathering images at the beginning, was Kapsul, which was created for curation. We used that as a way to start sorting the categories for how we eventually arranged the images in the gallery. So essentially, we were using cutting-edge, up-to-the-minute technology to put the show together.

TB: Wow, so much innovation! I want to come back to this idea about the different technologies that you all used to construct the show. But first I want to talk about how the show also highlights surreptitious practices people of African descent have deployed to resist oppressive forces, whether that's through

image-making or the use of various technologies. Can you say more about this and offer a few examples that illustrate this focus?
JJ: The book itself is such an amazing technology. So black folk writing, to start with, is foundational; and all of these particular spaces are rooted in the literary.

TB: Right, and there are so many authors represented in the show!
JJ: Yes, and that was something that was really key to the Schomburg's involvement. A lot of those books were from their collection. We also examined film. Look at something like *Daughters of the Dust*. It's brilliant, just brilliant. When Julie Dash uses moving image technologies to expose various types of traditional technologies from the culture that comes over from Africa that then situates itself within the Gullah people's culture—we can look at that as this idea of a haunted technology, how the spirit haunts technology. One of my favorite moments from that film is when the gentleman is taking the photo of the family and he sees the little girl who's not yet born. The future is literally haunting the present. So ideas about how we use various modes of technology, whether it's a cellphone or race itself as a technology—remediated technology stacked on top of each other—were very much a part of the show. Take, for instance, Manzell Bowman, who made the image we used to promote the exhibition (the mind-blown image). He doesn't even have a website. Instead he has an Instagram page, and he has thousands and thousands of followers. He's making this beautiful work on an iPad.

TB: Such beautiful work.
JJ: Or people like Stamford Carpenter, who hacks into an app on his phone to make all his cartoons and then downloads them. People are borrowing technology and hacking into it to change the ways it's supposed to work.

TB: I like the idea of hacking, and I want to keep going with that. In the exhibition text you and Reynaldo talk about the data thief who's drawn from the Black Audio Film Collective's *The Last Angel of History* of 1996. The data thief, the griot, the shaman, and the DJ are all kinds of hacker figures—key cultural figures that show up in one way, shape, or form in the visual and literary texts in *Unveiling Visions*. The show also, as you said, includes a range of objects from the Schomburg's archives. So in a sense, you and Reynaldo took on the role of data thief, griot, shaman, and DJ. But those figures also populate a lot of the works that are in the show. The DJ in particular is interesting because in hip-hop culture, DJs crate dig. They sort through records to find and play the

illest, most obscure, most body-rocking tracks to connect with their respective crowds of listeners. Can you talk about stepping into those roles and your curatorial practice as a kind of hacking? What was it like crate-digging through the Schomburg materials?
JJ: That's a great observation! You know, it's funny; I'm not trained as a curator. So I stumbled into it by thinking of curation as just another design problem. Design is my wheelhouse. But a lot of the practices we employed—utilizing digital prints for instance—came from curatorial exercises I had done making and publishing comics with Damian Duffy. The idea was that, well, a lot of things are popular culture materials; they're meant to be consumed. They are not precious in the same ways as the *Mona Lisa* by Leonardo da Vinci or *The Banjo Lesson* by Claude McKay. A lot of the people making this stuff are inspired by pop culture, by sci-fi, by Octavia Butler and George Clinton. These are the things fueling the fine art, if you want to make those distinctions. I don't because the work crosses high and low culture quite a bit. In terms of our curatorial process, it was the opposite of what we typically think of as curation. It was more of like a hoarding—like, okay, let's get as much stuff in here as possible!

TB: Right, instead of funneling or a refining—
JJ: Or a distillation. Isissa [Komada-John] brought that kind of finessed structure to the table, thankfully, [laughs] because we are data thieves. I was in a mental state where I just wanted all of it! That was the mode of thinking: a data thief collecting stuff for a time capsule to take somewhere or to pass on to future generations. So when Isissa came up with the idea to do the iPads as a kind of movable data screen, it was brilliant because it totally played into the sci-fi aspect of the exhibition. Even the way the Latimer/Edison Gallery is built feels like a capsule because it's round. It has the feel of a rocket ship, a capsule, of time travel. You can see through to the Schomburg's archives downstairs.

TB: Yes! That was so dope!
JJ: You can see Aaron Douglas's murals, so you can see the past as a reminder. But also what he was painting was very futuristic. He was already modernizing the black form. It is just mind-boggling how many connections were made—historically, visually—just from being in that space. There have always been folks borrowing from other traditions and remixing things, you know, and they become living indices for all of these historical moments and different things simultaneously. This impulse fueled the curatorial choices we made and the method by which we put stuff together.

TB: Very cool. Some terms that come up a lot in reference to this show are "Afrofuturism" and "black speculative imagination." Additionally, over the past fifteen years, there have been a slew of exhibitions and writings on these terms. Can you briefly define what these terms mean to you, and how this exhibition fits within this cultural milieu?

JJ: "Afrofuturism" is a term coined by Mark Dery, a white cultural critic who was trying to put his finger on something he had stumbled across. He identified themes such as black people in the future and technology, metaphors of alienation and displacement, and interviewed people like Tricia Rose and Samuel Delany to comment on this confluence as part of the piece of writing that features his definition. But even in the definition—he writes "for lack of a better term"—he leaves space for speculation. And we've always used our imaginations as liberation technologies, as storytelling, as speaking things into existence, analyzing technology that can actually give us freedom in a particular space. I think the oppressed always understand the systems better than the oppressors. So for me Afrofuturism is a node in an ongoing system of black speculative culture that has been used for generations to imagine a better space but also to actively create a better space. For instance, we closed *Unveiling Visions* the same day as the Black Comic Book Festival, created by Jonathan Gayles, Jerry Craft, Dierdre Hollman, and myself. When you entered that space, black people were the default. Period. Seven thousand of us in a space. So essentially through imagination we created a parallel universe where if you step up in there and you're anything else but black, you're not the default. It's pure imagination from the diaspora, whether it is scholars, artists, or people selling t-shirts; it is blickety [sic] black from top to bottom. And that is really powerful to me. The other thing is there are all these children who will never have to go through life not seeing themselves in the future ever again. I love that idea. It's a core element of the show, to empower people through their own storytelling. In thinking about the Black Speculative Arts Movement with Reynaldo, we wanted to untether ourselves from having to rely on other people's imaginations of us. So in *Unveiling Visions*, we wanted to show that not only are these people imagining an alternative past, but we're constructing the future by story, by art, by movement, by coding. These new constructions are why the idea of the data thief digging through the detritus of time and space and repositioning what blackness is radical to me.

TB: That goes back to the question of the design problem, too, on the level of form in the curation of the exhibition itself because what strikes me about *Unveiling Visions*, and we've talked about this before, is the fact that there is

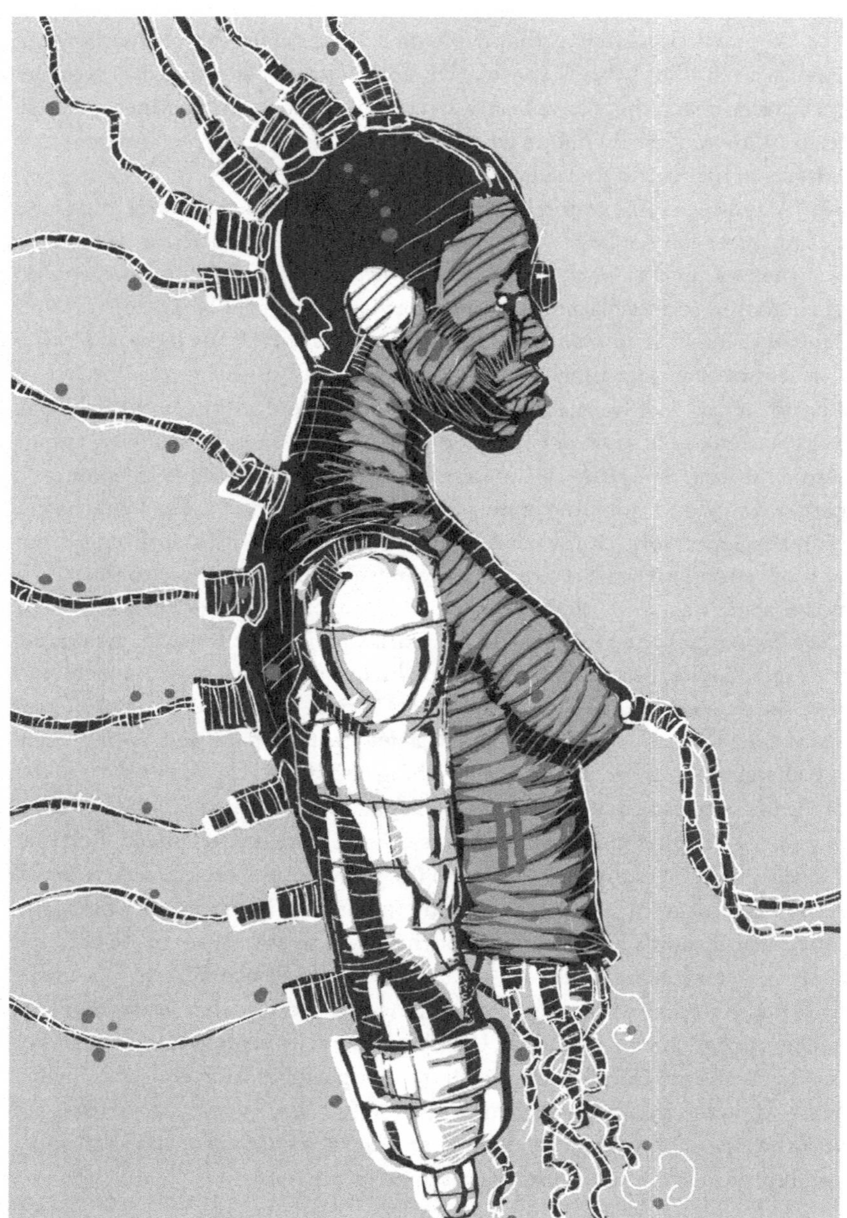

Electric Wet-Nurse X, from *Pitch Black Rainbow: The Art of John Jennings* (2014). © 2019 John Jennings, permission of John Jennings.

so much material culture represented versus this notion of fine(r) arts that appear in a lot of the other visual art exhibitions that have been staged about black speculative culture.

JJ: Right, we were really thinking about how libraries function . . .

TB: . . . and the hub for black archives is obviously the Schomburg Library, part of Arturo Schomburg's legacy.

JJ: Right, and *Unveiling Visions* is an extension of an archival project.

TB: Yeah, it's so interesting to think about how you all ballooned the notion of curating as collecting or situating or drawing refined connections between objects on display. Sure, there were things that aligned, and those connections were purposeful. But there were a lot of connections that were unexpected.

JJ: Yes, the objects speak to each other in a particular way when you're using the materiality of blackness distilled through a pop-culture lens.

TB: But it's the maintenance of an older kind of materialism within a digital or postdigital age that swarms with new materialisms, affect theory, and the idea that we're no longer of our bodies.

JJ: As a designer, one of the things I thought about in relation to that and your previous comment about curation, is space. People don't realize how much space labels and wall text take up. So we printed all of the information on to the posters. We controlled all the space. There were very few things left to chance. Also, we installed with magnets for an easy, clean install; we didn't have to worry about frames or shipping. What I love about it is the fact that it's virtual. So if we wanted to, we could mount this show in many locations simultaneously because of the ubiquitous nature of the digital. So not only are we hacking into how people curate shows and hacking into the archive, we're repurposing the digital—remixing. It was highly interdisciplinary, collaborative, and creative. I'm very proud of the show.

TB: It was a great show! Earlier we started touching on this idea of critical making without naming it. Critical making is central to your own practice, not only in terms of how you put the show together with Reynaldo and Isissa but also in the work you create as a graphic artist and scholar. Can you talk a little about your notion of critical making and how it comes to bear in the show?

JJ: As a graphic designer and illustrator by trade, I'm always thinking about the artifact, the deliverable, and the systems that produce that deliverable. That epistemology can be applied to almost anything, and critical making essentially is design thinking. It's thinking about the planning of a particular space or an intervention that often ends up being visual. It's not just, "Oh, I need a logo!" Why do you need that logo? How does it function? So I'll create a story, make an emblem, or design a costume, some visual artifact that answers these questions. Usually it's something that is going to create an object—most times it is—but we also investigate how branding systems work. Apply that to race, gender, or religion, and it gets really interesting. This thinking led me to what I call critical race design studies, a conflation of critical race theory, design history, critical making, visual anthropology—a mishmash of different ways to think about race and how it functions. Because we know race is a construct, but what are the blueprints? What does it look like? Critical making and visual thinking help us get at these questions and help me resist the hypercapitalist nature of design because I apply design tools to social justice issues, or a curatorial project in this case.

TB: Awesome. Okay, last question: What are your hopes for the afterlife of *Unveiling Visions*?
JJ: Well, it will have its own archive, and like a lot of shows it will live on through the exhibition catalog, a talking book to which I eventually want to add augmented reality. That was actually supposed to be a part of the show—we were planning to do an app called the veil in which certain artifacts would solely exist—but we ran out of time. As for the archive, the Schomburg is giving the exhibition posters their own space so anyone who wants to study Afrofuturism or anything and anyone in the show—

TB: Or black intellectual thought in general—
JJ: Right, people can visit the Unveiling Visions archive for that.

TB: That's dope! What an exciting contribution. Thank you!

King and Faith: Art and the Urgency of Now with John Jennings

BRIAN WATT / 2018

From *The Forum*, Grace Cathedral's flagship conversation series faith, ethics, and culture, January 28, 2018. You can learn more about *The Forum* and watch a video of Mr. Jennings's appearance at gracecathedral.org/forum. Reprinted by permission of Brian Watt and Grace Cathedral.

Brian Watt: Good afternoon, everybody. Happy Sunday, Monday's not here yet. I am Brian Watt, this is John Jennings, and I'm going to formally introduce him. Thanks very much for coming. We are sort of in the middle of a month where I've been thinking a lot about—well, we're coming on the end of a month where I've been thinking a lot about [Martin Luther] King and faith. I will admit that I will be turning fifty in June, which means that I was born two months after Dr. King was assassinated. So the reflections that I have been having in the work that I've done on KQED and also moderating some things for the MLK Foundation has me thinking of when my mother was pregnant with me. Two months to go in the pregnancy, and Dr. King is assassinated. She was a grad student in New York City. She would go on to be a school principal and work for the department of education. My father was in law school, and he would go on to be the managing partner of a civil rights law firm in the South. I'm from Charlotte, North Carolina, and so I've just been thinking about it, because I have kids. I have a daughter who was born, basically, a month after Donald Trump was elected president. I'm a journalist, I'm married to a journalist, and we're both journalists of color. So I, we have a lot of reflecting to do about how we're going to tell our kids about this time that we're in. In walks an awareness of John Jennings, someone who, you know, has found different ways to communicate about the times we're in but also about the past and the future. And we'll talk about that with him today in the context of the legacy of

Dr. King. So let me formally introduce John Jennings. He is professor of media and cultural studies and a cooperating faculty member in the Department of Creative Writing at the University of California Riverside. His work centers around intersectional narratives regarding identity politics in popular media. He's the coeditor of the Eisner Award-winning essay collection *The Blacker the Ink: Constructions of Black Identity in Comics and Sequential Art*. You'll see an image from that in the cycle here. The cofounder of the Black Comic Book Festival at the Schomburg in Harlem and cofounder and organizer of the MLK North-Cal Black Comics Art Festival in San Francisco and also SOL-CON, the Black and Brown Comics Expo at Ohio State. He was a Nassir Jones Hiphop Fellow at the Hutchins Center, Harvard University. I will forgive him for the Harvard part being a Yale man myself. Someone has to go to Harvard and some work and it was really good work. Please welcome John Jennings.

John Jennings: I didn't go there, I was a Fellow. [laughs] Thank you, thank you for coming too. It's really, it's seriously an honor.

BW: So I want to start with your story. I'm on my third career. I was a man in the theater, I was a man in politics, and now I'm a journalist. But I am really curious about how you got into work with images, design. So we need to know where you're from.

JJ: Right. I've been pondering that quite a bit just of late because of various things that are happening career-wise. And you know I work on a large spectrum of different types of projects. I mean from original comics work, but also I do a lot of critical analysis work. I do a lot of curatorial work. I collaborate a lot actually too because I think it's really an effective way to mentor and get more work out. So yes, I've been thinking about just career-wise where I've started and how did I end up becoming a media studies professor. My background's in art actually. I'm trained as a graphic designer and a visual artist, caricature artist, cartoonist, and book designer too. Most of the books I've worked on I've designed myself. So I'm from the South as well. I'm from Mississippi. I was born in Brookhaven, Mississippi, which is about an hour north of New Orleans. I was raised in a small, tiny, like, one-stop town called Flora, Mississippi, which is about fifteen miles north of the capital, Jackson. Our claim to fame is that is where the petrified forest is. Other than that, to think about when I became interested in images, I became interested in images super early, maybe when I was about four. A lot of people don't realize it's a type of literacy. It is a type of working-through, a type of problem-solving. I think a lot of times we get really caught up in this notion of old rote ideas about reading and writing, which is awesome, you've got to do that, right. But there's also, like, historical literacy, visual literacy, different modes, historical literacy that all encompass various modes of how we actually deal with humanity. And images for some reason, particularly when you look at comics are sublimated to this kind of juvenile space, but they're actually very symbolic and complex. That's the thing. So I was raised by my mother primarily and my grandparents. My mom went to Alcorn State University, which is another historically black college in Longhorn, Mississippi. And she ended up becoming a literature major. She became pregnant with me and actually did not finish and ended up moving back in with her estranged mother. And so that was really interesting, I guess, because I wasn't there yet. But it sounded interesting. So she always had her books around. Flora is a very agrarian tiny space; you know, it's extremely segregated. I was born in 1970, so of course there's still a lot of segregation in the space in schools and resources. And there still are actually. Mississippi is still a contentious space; let's just say that. So anyway, she always encouraged me to read everything right. My grandmother was a quilt maker and just looking at the things she used to say I think she probably was a root-worker as well. I think she actually did some conjure work and things that I used to think that were superstitious back in the day. Now from my research, now I think she probably was a conjurer, or she probably was working in that particular space. So you have that. I'm growing up in the woods, literally. When I say the sticks, if you say the term "the sticks" that's where a picture of my house would be, there in the dictionary. It's almost like stereotypical upbringing. Almost abjectly poor, in the middle of a cotton field, you know, that kind of thing. Severely financially challenged to say the least. But I had a lot of imagination. I started making art early, probably before I could actually write. And my mother had books around—psychology and illustrated books around, science—and she was a huge reader of science fiction, fantasy, and horror, you know, stories of the supernatural. And I just gravitated towards those kinds of genres super early. And I think, I didn't know I was becoming a graphic designer or a visual communicator at the time, but I was. There was something that attracted me to visual communication super early on. So I started drawing around the age of four.

BW: That's what I was going to ask. When did you start drawing, and when did you know you could draw?

JJ: Yes, it was around four. I had an uncle, my uncle Willie Albert, who at the time was an extremely talented artist. He could pretty much draw anything, and by this time my mother had given me my first comic book, little knowing that she created an obsession that would become my career. So for instance I was reading stuff like Greek mythology and Roman mythology and Egyptian and Norse mythology at a super early age. I was reading at an accelerated level super early. And she gave me my first *Mighty Thor* comic book by Jack Kirby and Stan Lee. And she gave me my first Spiderman comic book, my first Daredevil comic book, you know, Moon Knight, and all these wild characters. I was like, "Oh my goodness, these are like the gods and goddesses I was just reading about, but they're, like, somehow cooler." So I just started trying to make my own. And before you know it I was just drawing a lot. We didn't have art classes at the school, but I always had an aptitude for it. And so I went from there and did really well in school, but I actually did not go to college at first. I actually went to the military first because I was seventeen. I graduated early, I was valedictorian, but no one told me you should go to school. It was really tripped out. And I ended up having an accident where my foot was injured. I have a piece of steel in my right foot holding my third metatarsal together. And it turns out that our school actually requires you to take the ACT, and it turned out that I had a scholarship still at Jackson State [University]. So I was able to get a scholarship, but I was convalescing from my surgeries. I'm pretty sure I was the only freshman in 1989 at Jackson State that signed their scholarship papers while convalescing in a military hospital. So I was literally on the wrong path. It was like the universe—and so we're talking about faith, right? I would almost argue that God broke my foot and saved me from, not necessarily making a mistake but just the wrong decision. I would never say that going to the military is a mistake. I would say that it was a decision that I think was stopping me from my true destiny. And so when you look at it that way, there was something that was, that had realigned my faith, so to speak. So I did really well at Jackson State. I majored in art and had a minor in drawing. At the time I was working for the campus newspaper the *Blue and White Flash* as a cartoonist. I was kind of a hustler, so I made a lot of flyers for the Greek organization parties. That's how I made money. I used to call myself Up All Night Graphics. You could call me anytime, day or night, and I would actually make a flyer for you. I'd come out of sleep, say what you need, when's it going to be, and I'd draw it. I'd pick up anywhere from $10 to $12, $20 if it was a super rush. That's a lot of money on a college campus, seriously—especially, for someone who didn't have the wherewithal to have their own money. So from there I ended up doing some work at the *Clarion Ledger*, which was, like, the biggest newspaper in Jackson, in the state of Mississippi. And right out of school I was doing illustration work and graphic signage for the paper. But it just wasn't, I didn't think it was enough for me. I was still curious about what else I could do.

BW: At this point were you off to the side drawing the speculative, the supernatural?

JJ: Always, yeah.

BW: So this was something that was happening super early, while you were in college. I'm curious what, if you were able to display some of that work. And how the black experience, how your experience played into the work. But also how the community received your work. Like if you felt embraced because to me it strikes me as something different. And I would be curious to know how it was received by your peers.

JJ: Super early, yeah. Well, you know, later on, I think it started to become really well received. You know a lot of artists don't like to hear this, but you know you have potential to be really good at this. You always think that you're done. It's like, "Aw, I know I can draw; it's just raw material though." What are you drawing from? I think about drawing as not just mark-making, but literally drawing something out. How do you pull something into existence? It's a really powerful act because you're actually using something that's imaginary. You know lines don't exist in the actual space. You're using magic to a certain degree. Lines are like magic. And so, how do you actually pull those things out? And I didn't have enough experience to realize what type of things I wanted to do. I was still emulating things, and I think that's where you start. You start by tracing, you start by emulating things, and then before you know it you actually develop a style. A style really is a system of decisions. Whenever you choose to use a particular color to mean something or if you leave something out in particular or if you choose to use a particular medium, that's a system of decision-making that equals into a style. So I think I hadn't really developed that yet, at that time. I needed to go to school. I think after the accident, I felt like whatever thing that I was listening to inside of myself, I just went with it because inside of me I knew that I wanted to become an artist, but I still listened to other people and joined the military. That was a mistake for me. If I listen to what's inside of myself, then I think that is the way to go. That's what I did. So I have this job, it's the most money I've ever made in my life, and it's got benefits. It's a Gannet paper; it's with *USA Today* and all those papers. Little did I know that this thing called the Internet would come and totally demolish the print industry. Whatever was inside of me, maybe I knew. So I ended up going to graduate school at the University of Illinois, getting my first master's degree in art education. While I was there I applied to the MFA program for graphic design three times. The first two times I failed because I didn't know what graphic design was. I thought that it was interesting, and I wanted to know more about it. And so I was like, "I want to try for it," and they were like, "No, not good enough, no, not good enough." What I started doing was sitting in on their undergraduate classes, which was an excruciatingly embarrassing situation because to be, like, my age and sitting with kids younger than me who just could design circles around me. But I went backwards through their curriculum just because of when I started. So what actually ended up happening is I went into the program and became one of their strongest graduate students, and eventually I became the first African American professor to get tenure at the University of Illinois in the history of the school. And I was the first black chair of that program. The same one where they said I wasn't good enough to be at.

BW: Interesting how it happens like that sometimes.

JJ: Yes, exactly. And so little by little I actually ended up mentoring two more African American students who teach there now. One of whom is Nikita Thomas, who's the first African American woman to become tenure track in that program. So it's been a really interesting ride. In the middle of that I started doing research on what I would come to know as Afrofuturism.

BW: Which I'm going to ask you to explain because I know you will do a better job than I will. You know I did my homework; I was going to try to take you to Afrofuturism next.

JJ: Well, it kind of jumped off during my work at Illinois. I was doing my tenure work at the University of Illinois, which is like the early 2000s or so. I was doing these black cyborg images.

By a signal of hands, everybody know what a cyborg is? No, it stands for cybernetic organism. So have you ever seen the Terminator? Okay, he's a cyborg. So it's like metal and flesh. So I was thinking about and recently reread France Renound's *The Fact of Blackness*, and I was thinking about how an identity is created. You know, it's something we kind of—you're not born black; you become black. It's a designed object that encompasses you, and you say, "Hey, you're black; deal with that." You're not born white, it's something that

that's actually socialized, and it's a construct. And so I was really interested about that idea. So something that's constructed is like a device. So that could be the metallic part of it, the thing that's socialized. And the real part is the flesh part, the thing that we are inside. So those particular things are always, like, battling with each other. So that's why I did this series of like seventy to seventy-five images that just came out of me. I just could not stop making them. It was really surreal. I barely slept. They were digital images, and they just kind of flowed out of me over four days, seventy-five images.

BW: And how old were you at this point?

JJ: I was in my early thirties, I think. So it was over a decade ago, give or take. I was inspired by Japanese Manga and historical photography and things of that nature. And so I called the series "That Fact of Blackness." Excuse me, that's not true, "Matters of the Fact" because I was actually inspired by [Giuseppe] Penone's piece. When my friend Dana Rush saw the images—she's an Africanist—she saw the pieces, and she was like, "Those look Afro-futurist." And I was like, "You are making up words. I don't know what that is. What do you mean it looks Afro-futurist? I have never heard of that." But then once I did some digging, I realized, "Wait, this does relate to what people are calling Afrofuturism." The original term was coined by this cultural theorist, Mark Dery, in 1993. He has this collection of essays called *Flame Wars*, and they're all about cyber culture. There was this thing called the worldwide web that was actually being created in the early nineties, and people were doing a lot of discourse on how it functions and what could we do with it culturally. And what he did was that he picked up on a vibe of black-cultural production that he saw related to music and art and aesthetics and narrative. And so he wrote this piece called *Black to the Future* where he interviews Samuel R. Delaney, Tricia Rose, and Greg Tate. And so he postulates this notion of black techno-culture that actually utilizes futurity and technology in a particular way that is for upliftment of black cultural production spaces. Now, I actually typed something out right quick because I think there are some issues with how he defined it. One of the things—not necessarily an issue—it's an interesting thing is that even when he was postulating it, in his definition he puts "for lack of a better term." And I like that because it leaves possibility . . . It's almost like the antithesis of a definition—"for lack of a better term, I'm going to call it Afrofuturism." I dig that because since then, the resurgence of it fairly recently, we've been kind of dealing with various aspects of it "In an Afrocentric, speculative techno-cultural production system that privileges the political and creative needs of black people." So when we think about technology, we're not just thinking about the cellphone I just looked at or the projector projecting these images, we're also talking about extensions of ourselves, right? So religion, race, gender, and these different expansive things . . . history even is a technology because it gives us access to things around us. A more expansive idea around what technology is. And so how does an Afrofuturist aesthetic differ from say a traditional science-fiction aesthetic? This notion of nonlinearity of time, for instance, ancestral worship or the privileging of multigendered notions of leadership. So for instance, Afrofuturism tends to be a lot more womanist friendly. It actually is more about the equity of male and female aspects. Or the notion of time-travel or time not being this linear space or not even needing a time-ship. For instance, back on the back table I did the graphic novel adaptation of Octavia Butler's *Kindred*, which is about a black woman who is inexplicably teleported back through time to save her extremely racist great-great-great grandfather Rufus Weylin. But she has to do it because if she doesn't save his life, then she won't exist. But she doesn't use, like, a DeLorean or a Tardis, she actually utilizes some type of mystical connection, some kind of spiritual connection between them. And so this notion of the spiritual is actually, I think, an inherent aspect of black speculative cultural production, even more so than most other spaces. So around the same time that Dery was writing this book, *Flame Wars*, there's another gentleman named Erik Davis who wrote this book called *Techgnosis: Myth, Magic, and Mysticism in the Age of Information*. "Techgnosis" in his definition was about this really interesting connection between the spiritual aspect and the technological aspect and how they overlap. But guess what he ignores almost totally? Black folks. So it's like the way that we actually think about spirituality.

BW: Do you think he ignored it because . . .

JJ: I don't think he ignored it because there are references. He did a piece on Allegra the spirit at the crossroads, and he did reference the Egyptians. But as far as a more, deeper understanding of some of the more mystical aspects or supernatural aspects of black spirituality, he didn't really deal with it. And I don't think he just ignored it; I think it's just research. You know you have a time frame. And that's how I ended up working in Afrofuturism. And from then on, I just kept stumbling over people who were working in the same area. And so over the last decade or so it seems to be a massive resurgence of interest in black speculative culture.

BW: And when you say, just for everyone, "black speculative culture," I don't want you to spend all our time defining terms, but I think it helps people understand what you mean.

JJ: So anyone read any science-fiction or fantasy or horror? Anything outside of what people think of as reality? For instance, that includes fantasy work, magical realism work, or things that are kind of pushed against the boundaries of what we think are actually real. So when we talk about black speculative work, we're talking about work from people as early as, say, Zora Neale Hurston. W. E. B. Du Bois even wrote speculative fiction, by the way. George S. Schuyler's work *Black No More*—anyone ever read *Black No More*? It was written in 1931 by Schuyler. It's about a device that actually allowed black people to become white people. That's sci-fi that was written in 1931. If you go back even further, you're talking about stuff like . . . My colleagues Britt Rusert and Adrienne Browne, they found in W. E. B. Du Bois's papers a piece that I think was written in the early 1900s by Du Bois that was called *The Princess Steel*,[1] and it was a science-fiction, fantasy story. They found it in his papers and put it out in a collection of his work. So what is it about the notion of speculation and blackness that go hand-in-hand? And if you want to talk about Dr. King's work, for instance, anyone who knows the mountaintop that King puts forth, this mountaintop where everyone's equal . . . it's a utopic space. So if you pull out your GPS device, do we know where that mountaintop is?

BW: I don't.

JJ: I haven't found it yet. [To the audience] Do you know where it is? Is it close by? No, it's not a real space. It's a heterotopic space, dream-space; it's a liberation technology that he created as a metaphor to get us to think about what these future spaces could be. And that's really interesting to me. It's a black-utopia, or it's a utopic space for all of us, right? And building off of that, anyone know who Nichelle Nichols is? . . . Yes, she's Lieutenant Uhura. So at the time when *Star Trek* was on she was probably the only black face on mainstream television. Little do people know that she was really good friends with Dr. King. The story goes that she actually was getting ready to leave the show because she felt that she wasn't being effective in the space. And she was like, "Well, I'm tokenized a little bit." And she wanted to go back into Broadway. She actually was a very talented dancer. So from what I understand Dr. King and his family would watch the show every week. It was probably one of the only shows that he could watch with his family. And they loved it. He basically was like, "Please don't leave the show Nichelle because you represent us in the future. You represent us in the future, right?" And so he's already thinking about the importance of those types of scenarios. For a long time I thought her first name was lieutenant. I don't know who her people are. She's isolated; what tribe is she from; where is she from? I don't really know that much about that. I'm sure they built that up, you know. I'm not a Trekkie necessarily, but I'm sure they built it up over the years. But what I'm saying is that she was, like, a lot of those characters tokenized. But she represented an entire race of people, like for real, on television.

Audience Member: What about Avery Brooks? I think he's really a spectacular actor.

JJ: No, Avery Brooks is great, but let me—we're going to get there. But you're absolutely right, and there's one of his episodes where . . .

BW: Definitely glad you brought it up.

JJ: But we're talking about the connection between Dr. King and that particular space. No, not the whole canon, you're absolutely right. One of my favorite episodes . . . never mind, I'll geek out. Don't do that.

BW: I think that might be okay.

JJ: So that notion of black space that was something that I think King was very concerned with. There's a book called *Freedom Dreams* by Robin D. G. Kelley that talks about this idea that in order for you to move forward in any type of revolutionary idea or movement, you have to first imagine yourself in that future. You have to first have the narrative to imagine yourself being free, to actually moving forward. I would even put forth that the first true Afrofuturist was the first slave that said, "You know what? I don't think I like this slavery thing. I think perhaps I should follow that star, and I shall go because I deserve a better future," that kind of thing. You know you think the people that actually migrated on faith, our ancestors, up from down south to the promised land, which would be Chicago, the south side, or other spaces like New York. They were dreaming of a better future. They were actually moving on not only their own actions, but the things that were going to affect their future generations. We deserve better than this. There's got to be something better than this. So the idea of pondering the future is something, I think, that has always kept our people going forward. Everyone who came to this country—well, we were brought here, but you know what I'm saying—it's about the dream of a better life.

BW: Let me ask you about the image of Dr. King as it appears in this kind of work. You have just broken down how he might have been his own Afrofuturist; that was very powerful for me. But I'm curious when the Afrofuturist designer, drawer, and artist actually sits down and starts to work with the image of Dr. King, what's that like? What are pitfalls you try to avoid? What do you worry about when you present his image in this kind of work?

JJ: That's a great question. We actually did a giveaway book that was part of the Black Comix Arts Festival, for the first one. It was in partnership with the BAART. And so we got this idea that we wanted to actually have our character Kid Code who's on one of these pieces, a hip-hop time traveler. If you could imagine Doctor Who mixed in with African Bambada and Green Lantern, so he's a time traveler. Basically, we set up this idea that these people were being kept in this kind of stasis, and they were on a train because we wanted to relate the idea of a freedom train to BAART. They were paying for it, and they had to connect it. We wanted this idea that they needed the oratory skills, the power of Dr. King's voice to wake up these people and save them. In order to do that Kid Code and his associate Roxy Clockwise had to travel back through time before he became the Dr. King and actually have him save these people. It was trippy because we definitely wanted him to look enough like himself. A lot had to be caricature. You want to be respectful of his image. Cartooning is about abstraction, it's not necessarily about representation, and it's about connecting different types of symbolic communication. Comics are very surreal, and they're very abstract. So that's the thing we had to play around with. But utilizing him in that way, I think we did a great job of respecting his legacy but also playing off of the fact that he is still affecting the future. The thing about Afrofuturism is that it's always about co-presence. All these things altering, time collapses. A really Afrocentric belief is that your ancestors are always with you.

Anyone ever seen this film called *Daughters of the Dust* by Julie Dash?

Audience Members: Yes.

JJ: You remember the part where the little girl is haunting the present, but she's actually not born yet? She's the ghost of a baby that is yet unborn. I just got chills just thinking about that; it's beautiful. It's about the decision-making process that is happening that is affecting the future. Most of the best time-travel stories are about the ripples, ripples in time. How do you know when you change something; how does it make other things happen?

[Referring back to Kid Code and Roxy Clockwise] And so at the end of it because they had the power to, they showed him the mountaintop in our story. So when he [Dr. King] comes back and he's talking to his kids and his wife Coretta: "You know I had this dream." And they walk off into the sunset. Basically, that was a really interesting piece.

Now, there was this episode of the second—no, the third version of *The Twilight Zone* with Forest Whitaker as the Rod Sterling character? I don't know if you've seen it, but there was an episode that Eriq LaSalle did where he actually had the chance to save Dr. King or save this child that would eventually save his own life. And he had to choose to save the child because he had made this connection to this child. If you ever get a chance to check it out, you could probably find it on YouTube or something. But when I saw it, and this was something that he wrote and directed—that particular version of *Twilight Zone* is horrific, by the way; the best thing about it was that episode. I'm sorry Forest Whitaker, but it wasn't that good. But that episode just stuck with me because it was talking about in order for certain things to actually transpire sometimes things we think of as negative or traumatic have to occur.

BW: Like when you injured your foot.

JJ: Like when I injured my foot. Exactly. Actually, if you've seen the recent Dave Chappelle show he talks about that too and about the Emmet Till case as well. So we try to be respectful, but also know that there are only a few images of Dr. King that we can use. And so a lot of times you have to extrapolate from those things. And a lot of times you are imagining based off of the images that you're seeing—what he would look like?—that kind of thing.

BW: One of the running slides on this rotation here involves . . . is it a Doctor Xavier King or . . . ? I was curious about the story behind that.

JJ: You're curious about that piece? Right. Anybody read comic books in the room besides me? So you know who Jack Kirby was? And you know Stan Lee. Pretty much anybody who's seen a Marvel Comic's movie knows who Stan Lee is. He's always the little old guy who's in every movie. He cocreated the entire spectrum of characters from like Spiderman to the Fantastic Four. A lot of people didn't really know who Jack Kirby was though. Jack Kirby was this kind of silent partner, always in the corner chomping on a cigar, creating work. He cocreated everything from, like, Captain America to Ironman to the Avengers. So me and my friend Stacey Robinson, we were talking about the fact that *The Avengers* movies had just made about a billion dollars—that's right a billion with a *b*—and how Jack Kirby's family was like, "You know what my father did for you was like work-for-hire, but what do you think about maybe breaking us off a little remuneration for our father's creations?" And Disney/Marvel was like, no, they were not going to do it. And so most of the early comics' creators in our country were Jewish, either Jewish immigrants or sons and daughters of Jewish immigrants. And so Jack Kirby's real name is Jacob Kirtzman; Stan Lee's real name is Stanley Lieberman. A lot of them waspified their names to fit in and a lot of times the only things that these Jewish teenagers could get were jobs with comics. Early on, comics were considered to be very low—actually above, a couple of steps above pornography. (Sorry, did I just say that in a church? Sorry.) It's the truth. It was not looked at as a very reputable position. But what they did was that they took this kind of low form and made it into something great. They were geniuses; they were creating entire worlds. And for them [Disney/Marvel] to say, "No, we're not going to give you anything *even though* we just made $8 billion." I mean, there's a difference between the law and what's right sometimes. So me and my friend Stacey were like, "Man, they're treating that brother like he black." And then were like, "We might as well call him Black Kirby—oh, wait a minute, that could be an interesting idea." So we created an entity that we started creating work through that examined Jack Kirby's aesthetic through an Afrocentric lens. And Black Kirby started making this swath of work. For instance, there's this film coming out in a couple of weeks called *Black Panther*—I don't know if you heard about it? (Black Panther was created three months before the Black Panther Party started calling itself the Black Panther Party. Did you know that?) It [Black Panther] was created by Jack Kirby and Stan Lee, two Jewish men. Jack Kirby said, "I have a lot of black friends, and I want them to have their superhero. I want them to have a character too." So they actually created this character to uplift African Americans. And some would argue that they could have created an African American character to do that, but they created this idealized African king. And so we were like those types of things we made more explicit. We actually have an image that Stacey did of Huey Newton sitting in the chair, the wicker chair, but it's T'Challa, the Black Panther. So we're actually making that connection more explicit. So this is the piece that you're talking about [referring to "The Uncanny Kingsmen"]. Some people would say that when they created these characters that Dr. King was an example of Xavier and Magneto; his villain was Malcolm X. Now, I mean that's a very contentious thing, and it's a retroactive continuity thing that they did as it moved along. Actually, Magneto was just a megalomaniac. But Black Kirby was like, if we're making this alternative world, what if it is true? So we actually started making these—I call them arti-fictions instead of artifacts—fake covers and postulations on things that could've been. That's what Black Kirby started doing, and that's where that came from.

BW: I think we've reached this point where someone might want to talk about Avery Brooks. This is where I was asked to open it up to the audience—if anyone has questions. I obviously would like to hear a little more about your anticipation of the *Black Panther* movie, but we could come back to that. If anyone in the audience has a question for John Jennings we'd love to have it. If anyone is curious . . .

[From the audience I used to read not just Marvel but DC Comics and also because of the person of color was like we didn't have any heroes and heroines. Only in comic books. Begins to refer to the issues with the Tarzan comic books and all the cowboys, Tonto, The Cisco Kid. Continues to give a decade by decade rundown of depictions of black characters in comics, then asks Jennings if he could talk a little about the slides of his artwork that's been streaming behind them in reference to historical figures and real people like Shirley Chisholm]

JJ: I read everything—problematic, spotted around. A lot of my work has been about digging back through aspects of history and re-presenting things, not representation but re-presentation. One of the aspects that I created about Afrofuturism—anyone familiar with the term "Sankofa"? Sankofa is a West African term; it literally means "go back and get it." Or it's no shame to go back and get something that you left and bring it back to the front. So I posited this idea of Sankofaration, which is like narration and Sankofa spliced together, so I've been actively trying to go back and get the things, some of the things that you've talked about graphically. For instance, Larry Fuller, who lives in Sacramento, was one of the only three African Americans in the underground comics' movement, along with Grass Green, who created the first black independent superhero in 1970 called *Ebon*. It was only one issue created right here. A lot of people have never heard of this man. But I've actually had the honor to become friends with him, and I want to take this character and re-present it and update the character and expand upon that character's adventures. A lot of things around Afrofuturism and black speculative culture is going back and trying to show new generations the power of the narrative, the power of the types of things that have come before—that you're not by yourself, that you're not isolated historically, that these things are powerful and they have meaning and resonance outside of just being these artifacts that have no connection to your heritage. These are the things that we're really concerned with. And so when I'm creating these conferences, like co-creating these conferences and things of that nature, basically, I'm trying to restart or realign the idea of black subjectivity. And what I mean by that is a lot of times when we think about stereotypes, stereotypes are about fixity, in fact. And I say this all the time the root word of the word "stereotype" is the word "stereo," which is Greek for "hard or fixed" and functions as ways of trapping you in a particular way. So when you talk about something that's subjective it's more mutable. So by creating spaces where, like, black kids come and can see artists of color from various backgrounds, from various faiths, or what have you, they're actually seeing themselves reflected back at them, and that's an extremely empowering thing. There are a lot of people who are in power who take that for granted, so over the last few years we've actually, literally, realigned the psyches of like over forty thousand people. So you're talking about kids who never have to know what it's like to not be central to a story, and that's an extremely empowering thing. And so they can't; they won't allow themselves hopefully to become stereotypes. They'll actually create things and relate back to these types of images that they're going to know about. I can see some of these kids who are going to be like twenty-five years old saying, "Remember when we used to go to the BCAF [Black Comix Art Festival], and we would see all these images of everyone being there, having a great time? I want to do something like that." You know, we didn't have that coming up, and I know it sounds like everybody says, "I didn't have that; we didn't have that this internets," you know what I'm saying? [laughs] But you know, it's these types of images I want to make. I want it to be about joy and our pain and about our historical connections to all these figures like Jimi Hendrix, or what have you, that I grew up looking up to. You saw an Angela Davis image up there right? Angela Davis is one of my heroes. I almost flipped out when I met her; she probably thought I was a crazy person. [laughs] I was like, "You're Angela Davis," and she was like, "Yes, I am."

BW: She probably gets that a lot.

JJ: Exactly, or Sonia Sanchez or Amiri Baraka or you know all these amazing people that throughout history are superheroes. I mean you think about it, like, everybody had a picture of Dr. King, probably J.F.K. and white Jesus right on the wall. That was on my grandmama's wall as well. And so these are our superheroes; these are avatars; these are people that we look up to. They help build a sense of community and history through the imagery that we see.

Yes sir . . .

Audience Member: Thank you for being here. You talked about DC Comics and in seventh grade when John F. Kennedy was assassinated, a year later I went to a Roman Catholic school in the Midwest, and we used to get a monthly comic book called *Treasure Chest*. And in 1964 one of the series in there was the story of a black man called Pettigrew, who ran for president of the United States. Talk about black-futurist.

JJ: Really?!? Sorry continue.

[Audience Member Briefly makes the connection between that story and president Barack Obama being elected.]

JJ: I never knew. I have never heard it. I wonder if it's part of, like, the golden treasure–golden key stories that were coming out of . . . from the east coast. Hmm, I am not hip. But the fact that that existed. See that's what I'm talking about; that's extremely powerful. For instance, do you guys know Tom Feeling's work? He did—he's most famous for this collection of images called *The Middle Passage*. Beautiful images, black-and-white images. He did a comic strip called *Tommy Traveler*, and it was about a little black kid who was reading black history books and he would time travel through the stories and go and meet these really famous historic people. And they have collected his very rare comic strips into this little book. And I managed to pay a lot of money for it, but I managed to get it because it's an artifact of our history. A lot of people don't know about Orrin C. Evans and his brother; they created the first collection of black comics in 1947. It was called *All Negro Comics*, and it was a collection of black images by black cartoonists. It was the only one that they did, and they never got a chance to do a second one because . . . let's just say that certain parties were interested in them not doing it. Let's just say that. So there's only one issue, but you could still find it because it's public domain. So you can actually still find it on Amazon now. Someone republished it, but this is part of our history. Or for instance Jackie Ormes, who was the first black woman to actually have a syndicated cartoon strip. There's a book about her by Nancy Goldstein, and she [Ormes] is getting inducted into the Will Eisner Hall of Fame this year. That's really amazing. And Will Eisner, he's like the Marshall McLuhan of comics to a certain degree. But he's like one of our top cartoon heroes. Isn't that great that she is finally getting inducted into that?

Yes sir . . .

Audience Member: I was just thinking Aaron McGruder and his cartoon Boondocks.

JJ: Oh, do you mean what Aaron McGruder is doing? McGruder's next project is a speculative fiction show called *Black America* where black people get reparations. It's going to be an Amazon show. That's going to be his next project. Oh, and he also did this satirical show called *Black Jesus*. I'm curious about what he's going to do with the *Black America* show though. But that's his next project. And to your point about Avery Brooks, you're absolutely right what an excellent, excellent portrayal of not only a black protagonist, but a black family and generations, like his father was there.

Do you remember the episode called *Far beyond the Stars* [from *Star Trek: Deep Space Nine*]? Well, here's the thing; I show it to my students. I teach Afrofuturism classes and stuff, so I always show this because Captain Sisko, he's having these visions where he's imagining himself as a 1950s black science-fiction writer. And so he's going back and forth through time, and it's a brilliant episode. So it's essentially about all the types of discriminatory practices that are happening to him in the past, but it helps him work through an issue in the present. It's a really brilliant episode. If you ever get a chance check it out. It's heartbreaking, but it's also just really hopeful and beautiful. . . . You know representation has changed a lot. There's obviously an uptick in people of color across the board in various types of speculative fantasy work and all kinds of things. You know, it's changed a lot. There's still a lot of stuff to be done, but, man, it's a very different landscape right now. And I'm very hopeful actually. I think even though *Black Panther* is a super-corporate property, it's owned by Disney, who owns Marvel, who now owns Fox, but there are so many people excited about this film. Okay, this is so silly, but you know like on Saturday morning you would see the toy commercials? They just put out a *Black Panther* toy commercial with a little Asian kid and a little black boy and black girl pretending to be Black Panther, and I watched that thing about seventy times. And I got really misty-eyed about it. What I'm getting at is representation matters. And so these kids are actually able to pretend to be this character. I think that what's happened is even though this is a hyper-corporate entity—let's not forget that—this is Disney; the mouse don't play. But a lot of people have actually recolonized Wakanda. Wakanda is a fictitious African country, but we've actually recolonized it with our imagination and our hopes and dreams. Isn't that interesting? Seriously, people have totally snatched it from this corporation. They don't care. You know how many tickets I bought? I've bought like, I think, twelve tickets. I bought some for my wife and my family, and I'm paying for Uber to take our nieces and nephews to the opening night to go see it—seriously, because it's important for them to see themselves like that. That's them. That's reflected back at them. That's extremely important. There was this meme going around of this young man, and he hugs the Black Panther poster. And he was like, "Oh my God, white people that's how you feel every day? This is how you feel every day?" And you take it for granted. Same thing for any person in power, you don't know what it feels like to not be represented because it's like breathing. And so he was like, "Man, this feels great." And now for it to be breaking records already and it's not even out, not to mention the *Black Lightning* TV show. Have you all seen the *Black Lightning* TV show on the CW? It's pretty good, and it's already breaking records for the CW. That's what happens when you actually—if you enable everyone to dream with you, you change the world. And at the end of the day I think that's what Dr. King was trying to get at with that mountain top reference, that if you allow all these different things to happen we move forward, as a people together. We rise or we fall together. And I think through these different types of narratives we can imagine those spaces and then bring—through imagination, inspire us to move forward. So for instance, all these kids that are seeing Black Panther and seeing Black Lightning and seeing the Falcon and seeing Misty Knight they can become their own superheroes and then push together. Narrative is how we fight back against these things. We've always used stories, dance, and all the different cultural production aspects to overcome. That's a song I used to hear in my church.

Audience member: What black stereotypes in film and television that Jennings is not happy about?

JJ: I think that traditionally there have been resurgences of constructions of what a lot of people call the black buck stereotype or the angry black man stereotype or the thug stereotype. For instance if you look at a lot of nineties-era films around these kinds of gang-sploitation films like *Menace to Society*; some are better than others, but I think recently when I saw *The Shape of Water*, I

CRITICAL RACE **DESIGN** STUDIES

An interdisciplinary design practice that intersects critical race theory, speculative design, design history, and critical making to analyze and critique the effects of visual communication, graphic objects, and their associated systemic mediations of racial identity.

An interdisciplinary design showing critical race design studies. © 2019 John Jennings, permission of John Jennings.

have some issues with Octavia Spencer's character a little bit. I love that film; don't get me wrong. I am a huge fan of Guillermo Del Toro. I think he's one of the finest filmmakers working right now. He's very good; it's a brilliant film. I did think that Octavia Spencer's character seemed to be an extension of the protagonist's whims and her voice and not necessarily having her own agency and maybe that was intentional because it was a 1950s-era film—you know, it was talking about how blackness is shown in the 1950s. But did she have to be cleaning up? And also how her husband was shown as being a cowardly man and not supportive of his wife. I'm sure there are a lot of husbands that are like that. But here's the thing, though, when you actually have a spectrum of different types of representation . . . for instance, I was a fan of *All in the Family* and crazy Archie Bunker. That dude, man, it's a good show. I am a fan of *Married with Children* and even if you look at the cartoons like Homer Simpson, but you can't have all those negative-oriented stereotypes without having a *Father Knows Best* or *Leave It to Beaver* or this spectrum, this continuum of really positive representations of people to get to the point where you can actually show humanity. So we can't really afford to have super-negative images at the moment because there's not enough out there because people are lazy. People don't do research—I'm sorry—unless you're a researcher. If you see something on television and you don't know someone who's gay or black or Chinese, you'll accept those stereotypes and not do anymore digging. That's just how we do; we're too busy to do anything else. So I think for the most part the stuff that I've seen . . . I have seen a lot more care and creating an entire person. Because a stereotype is a thing but a true character, you love them; you hate them You want to know more about them. You know, a great character even though he's a villain, Mr. Glass from *Unbreakable* by M. Night Shyamalan—that is my favorite M. Night Shyamalan character. That is a great character because you understand why he became a villain. You understand why he's traumatized. You can see he's a person and he's brilliant, and his wrath is present right under his little purple coat. He's an amazing character. Even though he's killed a lot of people in the movie you understand why he does it to a certain degree, or you may empathize with him. And that's a character. So I want more of that to happen because we deserve it. Everyone deserves to see themselves in a society that they participate in. We deserve it.

BW: Should we thank John Jennings?

JJ: I really appreciate it. Thank you so much. I hope you enjoyed it. Thank you.

Note

1. Du Bois's work The Princess Steel found by Rusert and Browne that Jennings mentions is in part inspiration for the title of his imprint Megascope for Abrams ComicArt. Megascope was believed to be the title before The Princess Steel and is featured prominently in the story.

Black Panther Brings Afrofuturism to the Big Screen

CHRISTOPHER LYDON / 2018

From RadioOpenSource.Com, March 1, 2018. http://radioopensource.org/the-world-of-wakanda/. Reprinted by permission of Radio Open Source.

I'm Christopher Lydon, and this is OpenSource. *Black Panther*, the movie, is heading toward $1 billion at the box office on just its third weekend. Already it seems that commercial success is likely *not* what *Black Panther* will be remembered for. It is a grand coming-together of African American cultural production. The story in it is a mix of myth and magic in the made-up African nation of Wakanda. It is a technologically advanced society in a land that never got colonized, and it holds the world's only big deposits of an all-powerful mineral element, vibranium. With its vibranium Wakanda could, if it chose, take over the planet . . . Wakanda is an immense showcase of black agency and so is this movie *Black Panther*, in all the arts: writers, actors working off fact and fantasy, imagination, and history and tough-minded politics, too. The talent ranges across the board . . . In the stunned aftermath of watching it, not least of the marvels about this movie is realizing that Black Panther, the character—and a lot of his immense fan base—is built on the culture of comic books that lots of us have never read. So this hour's inventory of Black Panther first impressions starts with those drawings going back even before the Marvel Comics series that began in the 1960s. John Jennings leads the way. Prolific in comic books and illustrated novels—like Octavia Butler's *Kindred*, for example—Jennings grew up drawing in Mississippi. He's professor of media studies now at the University of California, Riverside. He's dedicated his new anthology, *Black Comix Returns*, "to all the little black boys and girls who never have to know what it's like NOT to see yourself as a hero, as subject, as vital to the society you live in."

Christopher Lydon: In conversation with John Jennings this week he said this story is not about the numbers.
John Jennings: This film hasn't even opened in Japan and/or China yet. Yeah, there's no way it doesn't make a billion dollars, maybe almost a billion-and-a-half dollars worldwide.

CL: I'd love you to take us into the world, the politics of it, the art of it, in a sense the musical, the cosmology, the religion.
JJ: African Americans in this country have been thinking about the future or about speculation around race and identity since the beginning. W. E. B. Du Bois wrote science-fictions stories, right?

CL: Oh, I didn't know he wrote short stories.
JJ: Yeah, he has a whole collection of them. To me the first Afrofuturist, collection of Afrofuturism were the first slaves who said, "You know what? Let's get the heck up out of here." Think about the great migration. Chicago was Wakanda to people from the South. I'm from Mississippi originally, so imagine trying to put yourself into a better space where you're free, where you actually have agency, where your kids can grow up safe and healthy. That was Chicago and other places from the South where black people were met with nothing but turmoil and slavery and pain. So Afrofuturism to me gives us the space to kind of posit what if these particular types of spaces with disruptive colonial issues didn't happen, like a Wakanda. Or can we imagine a better space. So if you look at, for instance, music, Sun Ra, the experimental jazz musician, he posited, "Well if we can't have freedom on this particular planet, maybe space is the place." That why it's called *Space Is the Place*. Well okay, let's think about places where we actually can be free. As you know race and space are highly conflated. The black body becomes the index for bad spaces—the hood, across the tracks, these types of notions, sketchy neighborhoods, the dark-continent, you know, that type of thing. So all these different things are connected to this physical manifestation of race.

CL: I love it. So the artist challenges to sketch me an alternative space, sketch me out of this sketchy place.
JJ: Right, exactly. So you're looking at a space like Wakanda. So Wakanda was created by these two white Jewish men in 1966, who I'm sure were probably inundated with the politics of the time. And also we're talking about Sun Ra being in the same city at the same time too. He's actually generated all this funky music and things of that nature, like experimental jazz, and Jack

Kirby was very much in the know of pop art and all these different types of movements. And then of course you go down South, and Stokely Carmichael mutters, "We need black power in Greenville, Mississippi," the same year. You look on television in 1966, you have Uhura—you know, the first really major black space character in a science-fiction show. All these things are happening at the same time. Even though the Black Panther Party doesn't take its name from the comic book, it's interesting that these notions are created at the same time.

CL: John you're describing an alternative medium, a parallel universe that a lot of us don't . . .
JJ: That's exactly what it is.

CL: Don't know. How does it connect with, say, civil rights politics since the sixties or jazz or hip hop, for that matter?
JJ: It connects quite a bit. Isn't it interesting that this element that they covet so much is essentially an index for sound? It's called vibranium; it collects and redistributes sound. So think about what that means as far as an index for oral culture, music and hip hop and jazz, as an element. Of course the sister movement to the black power struggle is the Black Arts Movement. I think that—what I've posited recently is what I call the Black Speculative Arts Movement. What I've seen is a resurgence of black art that is of a speculative nature, say, fantasy, horror, science fiction, what have you, that's actually fused with these anti-prison industrial complex movements. You know the movements around black lives in America because there are people on the streets protesting who are making science fiction–fantasy stories. So for instance, if you look at books like Octavia Butler's *Octavia's Brood*, you actually have a collection of underground activists who are writing science fiction about better spaces. There was this one that came out of Baltimore—that I can't remember the name of it now—that is actually positing a future Baltimore. So this idea of using this West African notion of Nomo, speaking things into existence and writing yourself into the future, this is what Octavia Butler talks about in her work too. I think, definitely, it's all connected

CL: Who are the real idea mongers, major players in this world?
JJ: There are a ton of scholars working in this area. We just did a symposium called Planet Deep South. We created this thing called Planet Deep South a few years ago looking at the fact that a lot of these Afrofuturists, writers and scholars, were coming out of the South. You know, Sun Ra was from the

South, Henry Dumas is from the South, Zora Neale Hurston. Even if you look at someone like Dr. King or Medgar Evers, these are people who are dreaming of a better future. They're all southern political leaders—William Johnson was from Jackson, Mississippi; Maurice White from Earth, Wind and Fire; even George Clinton, down South—all of these people are from the South. So they're trying to think about I've come up in this particular space, now how do I move forward? Now if you look at people from the Black Arts movement, like say, Amiri Baraka, Henry Dumas, or people like Toni Morrison, they're actually writing science fiction and speculative stories to talk about black politics. Henry Dumas in particular. A lot of people don't know him because he was killed at thirty-three by a cop in Harlem, but he was really good friends with Sun Ra. He was coming from a Sun Ra concert or practice in Harlem, and most of his work was about critiquing society through speculative fiction. You know I think that the rise of these particular characters has always been about the people underneath who are actually pushing for these things. You know this culture has been here for a long time. If you go to the Schomburg Center for Research and Black Culture in the middle of Harlem on the day of the comic book festival, which is the Friday and Saturday before MLK day, people are wrapped around the building waiting to get in to see, not *Black Panther* or black Ironman or Falcon or whatever, they're going to see black independent comic book artists. And everyone there sells out. So we are talking about a space where literally the ashes of Langston Hughes are buried in the foundation of this place. It's like peak blackness, MLK weekend, Malcolm X Boulevard, Harlem, all black everything. And it's Wakanda for those two days.

CL: I'm going to see you there next year, John.
JJ: Yes, oh my God, you are going to love it. It's a celebration of creativity. And these are all black independent comic book artists that we focus on in our book *Black Comix Returns*. We have entrepreneurs who are of color who are from various backgrounds, who are making comics day in and day out. We have people who are like—well, one of my friends is a bouncer. His name is Chuck Collins. He's a bouncer by night; he goes home and makes comic books. We have people who are waitresses and doctors, lawyers who have the talent who go home and make comic books. We have designers who design for a medical pharmaceutical company all day and go home and make comic books—this is what I'm talking about—who have this particular type of zeal and talent to actually go and have the skillset to make these things.

CL: Describe the ideas about humanity that animate this world.

Illustration for the short story *I Make People Do Bad Things* by Chesya Burke from *Sunspot Jungle: The Ever Expanding Universe of Fantasy and Science Fiction, Vol I* (2018). © 2019 John Jennings, permission of Rosarium Publishing.

JJ: See, this notion about the black body being safe in America hasn't really been the case. Black people in America were directly connected to three different spaces: the slave ship, plantations, and the grave. Those were the only three spaces we were supposed to be connected to. We were disposable objects that became people after the Emancipation Proclamation. Let's be real about it. So Wakanda, this black speculative arts movement space, even the black towns that we were forced to create in the 1920s and were subsequently destroyed, like Black Wall Street. You're familiar with Black Wall Street—1921, Tulsa, Oklahoma, riot where the first time a town was bombed from the sky? It was a black town; it had six millionaires in it. That was Wakanda. Rosewood was Wakanda. And so what happens when these particular types of things happen to be free to be a kid and not get shot when a kid plays with a toy gun or to go to the grocery store and not get killed, that would be nice to have. And these are things that people take for granted if you haven't been treated in this fashion. White people and black people are constructed. These aren't real things; they're not real. There's no such thing. It's this weird thing about how race is constructed. I was not born black. I was socialized to be black because of the surroundings around me, because of racism and class. So to actually be free to drop these things would be nice in an Afrofuture where these things don't matter. But until then we just have to create these stories as ways to resist these "skin-cells," as I call them. We're just trapped in these little bodies, and then we make stories about them. That's what it is. I mean, race is just a story.

CL: Is there an Afrofuturism outside the American world, even in Africa itself?
JJ: Yes, and that's what we're watching. The next step is people from those spaces creating their own stories. For instance, there's a group of artists in the *Black Comix Returns* book that are out of Barbados that are making comic books. India, Nigeria, Ethiopia, Jamaica, that's exciting. You know people like [inaudible] who's making film. There are some things that are coming out of Nollywood, from the Nigerian film industry. You know, it's a very exciting time. I don't see it receding this time. We've been doing this work for ten years before *Black Panther* broke wide, and it's incredible. And I think people are seeing themselves in these spaces, pushing it forward, and saying that these stories matter and we have the means to get them out.

John Jennings on Adapting *Kindred*

JESSICA WEBER / 2018

From UCR Today, July 17, 2018. https://ucrtoday.ucr.edu/54529. Reprinted with permission of University of California, Riverside.

For graphic novelist and illustrator John Jennings, transforming Octavia E. Butler's classic *Kindred* into a graphic novel was both physically and emotionally draining. Jennings, a professor of media and cultural studies at the University of California, Riverside, created the adaptation with fellow scholar, graphic novelist, and longtime collaborator Damian Duffy for Abrams ComicArts. Published in January 2017, *Kindred: A Graphic Novel Adaptation* debuted at number one on the *New York Time*'s Best Sellers list for hardcover graphic books and has received wide acclaim, garnering a Bram Stoker Award among other honors. Now, it is a finalist for this year's Eisner Awards for best adaptation from another medium. Jennings, who provided the illustrations for the two-hundred-forty-page book, called the eleven-month process "a small miracle." The work took a physical toll—Jennings injured his shoulder while working on the illustrations—but also an emotional one.

Originally published in 1979, Butler's story focuses on Dana, an African American woman who is transported to a pre–Civil War–era Maryland plantation, returning numerous times to help her white ancestor Rufus whenever he finds himself in grave danger. Trapped in the past, she experiences firsthand the harrowing cruelty inflicted on her own enslaved ancestors and, later, herself.

Turning Butler's book into a graphic novel presented Jennings and Duffy with several unique challenges, from figuring out how to truncate Butler's seminal work while doing it justice to the many aesthetic considerations involved in converting prose to a highly visual medium. "You can't go word-for-word with a comic book adaptation because they handle storytelling differently," Jennings said. "We actually had less pages to tell the same story.

Octavia was a masterful writer, but even with the terseness of her words, we still had hundreds of words that had to be cut and instead shown. That's the thing in comic books: you need to show, don't tell." To depict the time periods, Jennings played with the book's color schemes, muting the present day and making the past full-color. "Normally when you're doing flashback stories, the current day is vibrant and in color and the past is kind of sepia-toned, but we wanted to do something different," Jennings said. "We wanted to play around with the fact that in the book, Octavia talks about how vibrant and how real the past was and how bright and harsh it is, so we decided to do the opposite." For the scenes in the present, Jennings drew inspiration for the color tones from an unlikely place. "I actually sampled some of the colors from bruises and blood. The idea is that it's her blood relationship to Rufus that continues to pull her back. It's about family ties. That red is actually the color of what scabbed-over blood looks like."

In Butler's novel, time travel is more supernatural than scientific. To achieve this transition in the graphic novel, a subtle breakdown of the borders of the panels occurs. The lines become fractured and frenetic as Dana is pulled back and disappears completely when she finds herself on the other side of time. Jennings found the experience of immersing himself so deeply in slavery especially difficult, noting he is a descendent of slaves in the South. "I was crying physically onto the pages that I was drawing because it's so powerful and so prescient and so meaningful still today in the middle of the Black Lives Matter era. How do you get across visually the feeling of this book? My drawings were really manic and energetic, and they make people uncomfortable."

Despite the arduous process of creating the graphic novel, Jennings found the experience hugely rewarding, and it served as his first foray into mainstream work. "These are things that really effect black people in America still, the wages of slavery which I think our country is still paying, and you can see how that presents itself in our current political climate," Jennings said.

In graphic novel form, *Kindred* is offering new audiences a chance to experience Butler's thought-provoking work. "Some people who have never read comic books before have picked up *Kindred*," Jennings said. "A lot of the time, it's the first sci-fi or speculative story people have read because sci-fi is still dealing with representation issues with people of color." Jennings will be at this year's Comic-Con in San Diego, participating in several panels and attending the Eisner Awards ceremony on July 20. Known as the "Oscars" of the comic book industry, the awards are named for the pioneering comics' creator and graphic novelist Will Eisner. Jennings previously received an Eisner for

Merce, from *Pitch Black Rainbow: The Art of John Jennings* (2014). © 2019 John Jennings, Permission of John Jennings.

his scholarly work, *The Blacker the Ink*, but the nomination for *Kindred* marks the first time he has been nominated for his graphic novel work as an artist. "It's a huge honor, especially to represent Octavia Butler's legacy," Jennings said of the author who died in 2006. "I'm so glad we are a part of getting people to read her work and push her into the future. I'm hoping that if she's out there somewhere looking at us, that she's happy with what we've done, and we want to continue celebrating her." A softcover adaptation of *Kindred* is due at the end of July, and the adaptation will also be translated to Spanish, French, and Swedish, with those editions released in the fall.

John Jennings: Creating Social Change with Comics

RICKERBY HINDS / 2018

From the Creator State Podcast by the University of California, Riverside, August 6, 2018. https://creatorstate.ucr.edu/blog/2018/08/06/episode-1-creating-social-change-comics-john-jennings. Reprinted by permission of UC Riverside.

John Jennings: I live by the credo "artists are here to disturb the peace," which is a James Baldwin quote.

Rickerby Hinds: Yes.
JJ: I feel like, yeah, let's try to agitate as much as humanly possible.

RH: Welcome to the Creator State where we share stories of social innovation and entrepreneurship for movers, shakers, creators, and change makers. Each episode will celebrate success and failure, ingenuity, and the endless pursuit of knowledge. In a world that is increasingly visual, John Jennings has a gift for bringing words, people, and stories to life through his images. In this episode, we'll talk with the award-winning illustrator about his work on the graphic novel adaptation of Octavia Butler's *Kindred*, about pitching projects on the comic-con showroom floor, and the ways in which art allows us to explore how the past continues to influence the present. We are recording today's episode at the Center for Ideas and Society at the University of California, Riverside. I am your host Rickerby Hinds. Welcome to the Creator State. My first question is, if someone was to ask you what you do as a creative, what would the answer to that question be?
JJ: That's a great question. I think primarily I tell them I'm an artist. I think the media that I use are very interdisciplinary and varied. I think overall,

though, I was born as an artist. I'll die as an artist. I do writing and editing and all kinds of different creative enterprises, but I'm an artist primarily.

RH: Okay good. So taking off from the artist standpoint, what is your medium? If I say I'm an artist, my medium would be playwriting. I begin with the word. Where do you begin, and what is your zone of most comfort? That may or may not be the right word, but where do you want to land?
JJ: That's an interesting question as well. You're so good at this. Thinking like, when I talk to my students about media and about illustration in particular, I always say, "Stick to what you know and start with what's comfortable." So that's where I start, too. I'm an image maker primarily. I'm really into the iconicity of language. I used to teach classes around applied symbiotics and image making for graphic designers for many years. Before I started teaching here at UCR, I was an art professor. I taught design methodology, design history, these types of things around the economy of image. So I think primarily I'm an image maker, but you make images different ways. These days sometimes I say my medium is people. Because I think about . . . I do a lot of "cultural activism" around creating spaces, and so these days I've been doing a lot of collaborative work. And I really love the fact each person that we meet is like a universe. Each person is an opportunity to make something. So I think the mediation of being a collaborator is something I'm really interested in right now.

RH: Talk to me a little bit about when you say, "I love the idea of my medium are people." How do you take people and convert them into—
JJ: These artistic expressions?

RH: Yes.
JJ: I think that this is something I've kind of picked up from . . . Oh, what is the gentleman's name? Out of Chicago? Brother that's doing . . . He's a potter.

RH: Theaster Gates.
JJ: Yes. So I was thinking about this. I do some work in the community putting together ethnocentric comic book conventions, too. I cofounded probably the largest Afrocentric comic book convention. It was just in Harlem at the Schomburg Center. After I started doing this, I saw this interview with Theaster Gates and Bell Hooks, who is one of my sheroes. I just met her recently, too. She's a pistol. Love her. Anyway, so he was talking about the value of masters in fine arts. Like how when you're getting an MFA, it gives you a certain set of skills, a certain set of processes, that a lot of times think that you are just applying

to that one medium. He's a potter. He's a ceramist. That's the medium he starts in, but I think right now his medium is the community. His medium is buildings that he's reshaping. He's still a potter. He's still doing pottery. He's still making vessels, but he's actually utilizing his skillset he picked up as a master of fine arts and projecting them onto these older spaces in Chicago and rethinking them. So I started thinking about, "Well, I'm kind of doing the same thing." I'm still doing graphic design, but I'm actually collaborating with people, creating spaces, making partnerships with people, and designing or reimagining black subjectivity to a certain degree. Because over the last six years, we've actually created a space where over forty thousand or so children have come through the doors and have seen black independent creators making work, comics creators. Those are forty thousand kids who never have to know what it's like to not be central to a narrative.

RH: Wow.
JJ: So that's one thing. When I think about this idea of the mediation of people or people as media or people as stories, I think about that too. I think we're made out of stories. If anything, I'm an image maker, storyteller but an editor and a remixer, that kind of thing.

RH: Very cool. So I want to do a rough transition to *Kindred*. Why *Kindred*?
JJ: So Beacon Press, they have the rights to publish her prose work. So 2008, 2009, or so, they put out a call for teams to do a graphic novelization of *Kindred*. This is years ago. Black-and-white, fewer pages. I was at the University of Illinois Urbana-Champagne teaching still. This was around spring break, and my friend Damian Duffy, who I did the adaptation with, he finds this call at the last minute. And he's like, "Dude, they are doing a graphic novelization of *Kindred*, or they want to do it. We have to throw a hat into the ring, don't we?" I was like, "Yeah." Here's the thing, just like now, I'm always traveling around doing talks and my thing, so even over spring break I had three speaking engagements in three parts of the country. We decided to go for it, and so what happens is Damian cobbles together a pitch and puts together a really quick adaptation of the first scenes. I was literally jumping around from city to city, so what I was doing was drawing analog images large, sending them back to Champagne via FedEx whenever I hit another city. And Damian put together the pages in Photoshop. We were super excited about it, and we thought it was great. And we totally failed. Totally did not . . . We totally crashed and burned. We were so exhausted. I still did fine at my talks or whatever. We were like, "Okay, we failed but at least we tried." So it was decided that this book was

going to get made, and, low and behold a few years later, we're doing a talk about another book at San Diego Comic-Con. We had three other projects we wanted to pitch. I was like . . . Damian's in the air. He's on his way to San Diego. I'm already on the floor, and I have my trusty iPad. I'm showing images to people, and I walk up to Abrams ComicArts. I meet Sheila Kennan, who was at the time senior editor at Abrams ComicArts. I was like, "Yeah. Here's some things I'm working on. What do you think?" She's like, "Love your work. I think you'd be perfect for this project I'm trying to acquire. Have you ever heard of Octavia E. Butler?" I was like, "Why, yes I have. Actually, yes. She's a wonderful creator. What book are you trying to do?" She says, "I'm trying to do *Kindred*." I'm like, "Wait. What? What about the other graphic novel?" So what ends up happening is five months later, we're signing a contract to do *Kindred* with Abrams ComicArts. So it wasn't necessarily like we chose *Kindred*; it's like *Kindred* chose us. It circles back around to us, that kind of thing. I think it's one of her most beloved narratives because of the fact that it touches on so many different subjects. It's kind of like an alternative history story; it's definitely situated in sociology, women/gender studies, African American history, science fiction, horror. It just touches on so many different things. That's why *Kindred*.

RH: Okay.
JJ: We weren't like, "Hey. We're going to do *Kindred*." It's like, no. I was actually trying to sell other projects.

RH: *Kindred* came to you.
JJ: *Kindred* came to us. Exactly.

RH: I want to talk a little bit about the choices that you made within *Kindred*. Just talk a little bit about how those choices were influenced by, clearly, the novel itself but also by your own experiences and your own visual desires as far as storytelling.
JJ: Okay. First of all, comics is a medium all to itself. That's weird, but it's what comics is. And so it's an amalgam of word and image. It's sequential in nature. So it's almost like there's a theatrical aspect to it because you are all the characters. I like to image if you're thinking about it like the panels are very similar to seeing a play. You're dealing with all the costume design and stuff like that. It's a really interesting enterprise. It's a very exacting process. You want to get across the themes of the book as concisely as possible. This is a very important book to people. It's a very important book to us. Her fans

are rabid and Beyoncé Beehive–like. The sisters that are really into Octavia Butler, it's like, "You need to get this right." So it's a lot of pressure. At first, we wanted to do something that was more memetic, something that was more realistic, so to speak, but then the thing was how do you get across the effect of slavery and the horrors of these things through the illustrations? Comics are very symbolic in nature, and so what I started thinking about was other artists throughout history who utilize illustration to talk about trauma. So I start looking at a lot of people around the German-expression era. And particularly I centered a lot around people like Franz [Mazrio], Lynd Ward, and people like Kathe Kollwitz, in particular, who would beautifully do these extremely painful images around what was happening in concentration camps during the Second World War. I was trying to embody those types of feelings. The images have to be abstract enough that you can project yourself into them. Because like Butler talked about, she pulled back on the horrors of slavery. I really don't think we've actually seen a depiction of what slavery was really like, even if you look at something like *Twelve Years a Slave*. I thought it was actually pretty tame in comparison to the grotesque horrors of slavery.

RH: It's ironic that you just want to jump in, that you say Butler said she pulled back because one of the most compelling and powerful descriptions of what it was like to be whipped I found in *Kindred*.
JJ: The whipping scene—

RH: That description is the—
JJ: . . . When Dana is in the bushes hiding?

RH: Yes.
JJ: Yes. And that's . . . Actually, when I was drawing, that's . . .

RH: Yes.
JJ: Yes, and that's actually when I was drawing, that's an extremely . . . That was one of the pieces that we struggled with too because how do you get . . . And I think it comes across in the graphic novel, too. But while I was making the book, I was weeping onto original art pages.

RH: This is, yeah—
JJ: It's very difficult to cry onto your art and try to . . . You know what I'm saying? Oh my God.

RH: Yes.
JJ: It's very painful. So much in fact that I saved that part of the book for later to color because . . . See people don't realize you're embodying all these different types of emotions when you're trying to give form to—

RH: Absolutely.
JJ: So you start from the sketch, right? So we had to sketch out the entire book first to figure out what it's going to look like. The entire book has to be broken down into panels, sketched out. Then you draw it. So you're giving it more form. Then you ink it, giving it more form. Then you color. So you—

RH: So you're revisiting that space—
JJ: Over and over again

RH: Over and over.
JJ: It's a retraumatization of it. So actually, and this is—don't tell anybody—I have not actually read the entire graphic novel because of that. I read it in pieces and shards, and it was a project I had to get through. I read the book many times and listened to it many times. I would actually listen to the audiobook while I was drawing. So I was up to my eyeballs in slavery. We were enslaved by the book.

RH: Wow.
JJ: It was an experience.

RH: But I read also somewhere where you talked about this idea of momentary hope, and so I wanted to ask you, transitioning a little bit out of this traumatic place: How important is momentary hope for you in your work, and how do you assure that it exists in work that may be otherwise very traumatic, very powerful, very dark?
JJ: I do a lot of work around what I call the "Ethno-Gothic." That's my little terminology there.

RH: Yes. I was going to ask you about the term. Tell me about the—
JJ: Here's the thing. So *Kindred*, people keep placing into this term "Afrofuturism," which has been experiencing a resurgence over the last decade actually. The mainstream just kind of stumbled on it. "Wait. What is Afrofuturism? What does that mean?" And we've been dealing with this for a long time as

far as the black speculative space, right? I guess what I started thinking about was like, "Okay, well do you ignore traditional tropes around narratives?" You know what I'm saying? *Kindred* resonates more with a gothic narrative than it does with any kind of futuristic or sci-fi narrative. For instance, there's body horror, there's these weird ancestral tensions around the present and the past and the future, and there's the doppelganger. Alice is her doppelganger. There's this twisted romance story that's in it as well. It actually has all these trappings of the gothic. In fact, Butler talks about it as a grim fantasy. The other thing too is that there's this magical supernatural aspect of it. It's almost like Dana is haunting her own past. It's not like she jumps in a TARDIS or a DeLorean and just takes off and says, "I'm gonna go do a time travel." It's not H. G. Wells.

RH: Right.
JJ: There's an inexplicable, magical, haunted, uncanny connection to the past that draws her inexplicably to the past. And that's what's so powerful about *Kindred*, is that it talks about the idea of awe or cosmic unmaking of people through this weird machination, this technology called race or racism or whatever you want to call it. It's unnatural. That's what happens with *Kindred*. She's talking about how this actually still affects us today. That's why it resonates with us today because we can see that we really don't want to deal with those particular types of connections to racism in America. As far as hope goes, I think as someone who is a teacher I cannot do what I do without hope. It doesn't function. You're really trying to deal with future generations, and you're thinking a lot about what have I learned in my few decades on the planet and how can I impart that to future generations. That's the thing when I look out into my students, I need to actually get across the notion of hope because that's what we're working for, the future. Even in Butler's work, she's talking about, particularly in stuff like the *Parable* series for instance, it's a very dark narrative. It out-hungers *The Hunger Games*, but at the end of the day, the main character wants to save existence.

RH: Yes.
JJ: You have to have that. She creates a religion so you have to have that as part of the narrative, even when you're, as Toni Morrison calls it, 'playing in the dark' which for some reason I have an affinity for. I have an affinity for dealing with these darker subjects, giving them shape, but I think that's how you release that so you can get to that Afro-future. You've got to work through that stuff. You have to work through it. You give it a form. You give it a name. You know what it is. Then you can get rid of it. It's almost like the first thing

. . . It's in magic. It's like Rumpelstiltskin. "You said my name. You've got power over me now." That kind of thing. The fact that Adam named all the animals. That's powerful, right? So the idea of naming and claiming and giving something a reified form, you do that through these magical darker spaces or supernatural things that people are afraid of, that kind of thing.

RH: Now, let's get into the creative state of mind. In each episode, we ask our guest to share what's been on their minds, something they can't stop thinking about, a new challenge they're facing, or what's inspired them into action recently. We call it the "creator state of mind." What is messing with you right now as far as jumping into your creative space and telling you maybe it wants you to mess with it in the near future?
JJ: That's funny because whatever you mess with, it messes with you.

RH: Yeah.
JJ: It's interesting because I think that this notion of unpacking those horrors are actually something that actually I'm kind of obsessed with honestly. Because what's happened is I see how useful it is, the utility of it, and how scared people are to talk about these things and I'm like, "I'm not really scared of that stuff." I thinks it's because I came from Mississippi where racism is as natural as breathing. You are haunted, metaphorically, by Emmett Till's spirit on a day-to-day basis, and you get really resilient when it comes to these types of spaces. I see it, and I feel it. And I'm like, so okay, I have the proper mixture of weird things happening or very fortunate weird things happening. I think that's something I want to deal with. We're talking about these future spaces, and we haven't really dealt with the baggage of the past yet. It's like the Erykah Badu song, "Bag Lady."

RH: Yes.
JJ: That's how I look at these dark . . . That's how I look at *Kindred*. She's like, "We gotta still deal with this baggage before we get to the Afrofuture. What you talking about?"

RH: I was going to ask you about your mother because there's a cool thing that I saw about you speaking about how you and your mother watched horror movies together. First of all, I want to learn a little bit about these conversations you would have with her about what scared you and why. It's such a great way to examine these films, which clearly have translated into present-day questions that you must ask yourself when you're creating something.

JJ: It was cool. My mom and my grandmother too to a certain degree . . . I grew up, like I said, black, male, and poor in Mississippi, post–civil rights era. I was born in 1970. My mom went to Alcorn State University, so she was a literature major. And she had a lot of books around. I started reading and thinking at a super early age. I was off in the cut. I was in the sticks. Flora, Mississippi, is already an agrarian space, but I was in the most agrarian of that space. I just had my imagination, and my mom was my best friend when I saw her because she was usually working a couple of jobs to put food on the table. My grandparents were my main caretakers. My grandfather was my superhero. So my grandmother was full of what I thought were superstitions but in retrospect were probably belief structures that came from conjure culture or root work, something like that. She probably was a practitioner; I just didn't know it. She was always talking about haints and things of that nature. My mom was always into science fiction, fantasy. She gave me my first superhero comics, which became an obsession.

RH: Wow. This was in the seventies.
JJ: Yeah. She was buying me, like she bought me *Thor* and *Spider-Man* and stuff like that. She said, "Well, my kid's into art and he reads a lot so he might like these." I got more comics and stuff. We would watch these . . . She was always into scary movies and stuff. I started reading Stephen King too early, Edgar Allan Poe, that kind of stuff. I was really into these darker subjects, and I was surrounded. I'm in a forest, essentially, with a grandmother talking about spooks and haints and stuff. These things actually started affecting me earlier. They would show these old school horror movies Friday nights on our ABC affiliate. They even had one of those hosts. They would dress up like Elvira-style hosts.

RH: Yeah, oh okay.
JJ: I forgot what his name was. But anyway, he would do these second-run horror movies and stuff, and we'd stay up together and watch them and talk about, "Why was that scary?" "What did you think about the guy with the one eye?" Those types of things. So yeah, she let me watch a lot of stuff that I probably shouldn't. But she probably was scared too. But I liked it. Those, in some ways when I think about horror, I think about the narrative of the comfort of talking to your mom about this stuff.

RH: Wow.
JJ: I think it's a signifier for things that comfort me.

RH: So your point of reference to horror is a point of comfort.
JJ: Maternal.

RH: That's interesting.
JJ: It is. Horror is about us talking about the world, things that we don't want to deal with. Things that we are totally afraid—not just visceral horror—like one thing everybody is probably terrified of is going blind or losing a limb or something like that. It's terrifying because it's dealing with physical, visceral horror, but there's also these notions of dread that are very difficult to articulate. The thing that gets you in the middle of your stomach like, "I don't want to deal with that." My wife is totally terrified of centipedes. She's like, "That's too many legs for anything to have."

RH: At least she has a thought-out process as to what the dilemma is.
JJ: Hers actually, she doesn't have a logical fear. So I was like, "Yeah. Centipedes, they're messed up."

RH: They mad.
JJ: So a lot of times I'm talking about how do you talk about racism as a horror story? That's the only thing I think you can talk about it as from a black perspective. So one of the stories I'm working on right now, *Box of Bones*, which is Afrocentric *Hellraiser*. It's about these spirits that live in this box that punish people who hurt black people throughout the diaspora. The main character is this black woman named Lindsey Ford, who is working on her PhD at Berkeley. She comes across these stories about this box, and then she slowly realizes that they're not stories. They're real, and she's connected to these stories in some way. But these spirits, they're based off of black stereotypes.

RH: Nice.
JJ: So what I did, I took stereotypes, which are already monstrous and limiting and terrible already, and pushed them to spaces that spooked me out. Like, I have this one character called the Burden that is essentially like one of those . . . Have you ever seen those cotton sacks a slave would drag around? So imagine that filled with, like, arms and legs of slaves. And it inches around as it takes more legs and arms into it. It's about the utilitarian nature, the dehumanization of black people during slavery. So think about, "Okay, what does that look like?" And so these particular forms, I'm like okay. Well, how do I make those real? So essentially *Box of Bones* is about the Florida Evans moment when she smashes that bowl, in *Good Times*, on the floor. And she

said, "Damn, damn it!" How do you take that feeling of loss and suffering—in fact, one of the characters is called the Suffering—and put it into a space . . . How do you explain that?

RH: Wow.
JJ: Yeah. Yeah. And so art gives us the visual language to try to deal with those issues. That's terrifying.

RH: Okay. So, John, I understand that you are teaching a course here at UCR on *Get Out*, the film. I just want to ask you, what led you to deciding to teach a course on this film? And what have you discovered, or where has it led the class itself in your exploration of both the themes of the film itself but also themes that are embedded in your work?
JJ: Okay. Well, here's the thing. So when I was still at UB, that's the University of Buffalo, when I was still teaching there, I was teaching in graphic design, and I taught a class that I created called Applied Semiotics. Right? So I was thinking about the study of images and how you apply them through, like, a graphic design lens. Right? I always changed the theme. So one year we did this course called the Medium is the Monster. I was thinking about monstrosity and the grotesque and different aspects of it. So we talked about things, about otherness, about the monster being these internal fears. We talked about the demonization of female sexuality as being monstrous. It was like these really interesting conversations. And we showed these films. It was almost like a film series/class. And they did an art show. I could send you guys some of the images from it.

RH: Wow. Nice.
JJ: So I had been thinking about how do we talk about these things explicitly in a course like that? I'm a huge film buff. I own thousands of films. And I study intently how narrative works its way out sequentially, so I'm already thinking about these things. So I go to see *Get Out*, at the time though, I was still at Harvard because it came out in, like, November. So I had just started my fellowship. We were blown away by the story. I almost felt like Jordan [Peele] was inside my head. I was like, "These are the things that I think about all the time." Oh, my God. Okay, for instance, when he [the protagonist Chris] picks out cotton and puts it into his ear to protect himself, that's what I'm talking about. Black people have survived in this country by utilizing things that were created to destroy us—remixing them through our language and our art and

our dance and everything, and using art as a system of resistance. And that's what he was showing. He was like, you're taking things that are supposed to destroy you and you make it into a liberation technology. That, I was like, oh, my God. This is exactly what I'm talking about. So me and my wife went to eat afterwards, right around the corner from the movie theater, and I was like, "Man, I can't stop thinking about this film." I see so many layers to it. I see it resonating in things I'm already dealing with. I went back to my office, and in two hours I had written a syllabus. I wrote a syllabus. One of the things about the sunken place that's so fascinating is that race and space have always been conflated in our country. The sunken place is the Red Line South Side of Chicago. I come from the sunken place. Mississippi is a sunken place. You know, the other side of the tracks. I'm in a sketchy neighborhood. Those are sunken places. The prison industrial complex is a sunken place. Race and space have always been connected throughout our country's history. So when he [Peele] gives it a designated name, it becomes a signifier for all of those racialized spaces, to me. And you have conversations about those things. I was like, I want to teach a course on this, but I couldn't because I was still at Harvard. So I actually didn't get a chance to teach it until this past quarter. And so the students actually had to do a final project that was a critical making project and a written project about how they would imagine what the sunken place would look like as a cartographic representation, as a mapping system because if you got into the sunken place, you've got to be able to get out of it.

RH: Yes.

JJ: Right? So how do you help this brother get out? How do you get Chris out of the sunken place? And so students just went wild. They actually did these really interesting mapping images. And this is not an art class, but we do some critical making work in MCS. And I was like, well, let's work through this as a visual signifier. How do you talk about the visual manifestation of the sunken place? What does it represent to you? Yeah, but we're talking about how horror has always been a space of catharsis for black people. You know? Or a space where we can actually play around with these things. I talk about restorative justice politics through horror. I talked about the misrepresentation of black or African diasporic religion and horror. Like, stories like *Angel Heart*, for instance. You know, where voodoo is the devil. You know, that kind of stuff. I taught *Candyman* and these notions of how it talks about antimiscegenation and things of that nature. We had some really, really amazing conversations about these things. It's honestly been one of my favorite experiences because

Daddy Long Legs, from *Pitch Black Rainbow: The Art of John Jennings* (2014). © 2019 John Jennings, permission of John Jennings.

I think the students loved it. It was a special topics course. It was one of the classes that I want to actually get on the books. So it's Afrofuturism and the Visual Cultures of Horror, and *Get Out* was a central narrative. So I'm friends with Erika Alexander, who's in the movie, and she's Skyped to the course. And it was great. I was trying to get Peele to come, but that's around the Oscar rush, so it was a timing thing. But I think that in the future, I hope that he will come and do a talk with us. You know.

RH: It is always a valuable learning opportunity to take time to reflect. At the end of each interview, we like to ask our guests this: In hindsight, what is something you wish you would have known when you were starting out?
JJ: That your biggest competition is going to be probably just the amount of time you have. Don't squander your time. I always tell my students one of the biggest lies ever told to us is that time is equal to money. Time is timeless. Time is time. Money is money. Money is worthless. Time is all you have, and so what are you going to do with that time when you're here on this planet, in this particular plane of existence? The other thing that I would tell my younger self is don't compare yourself to other people. One of the things that actually . . . I stopped drawing comics for a while. I hate that. It's embarrassing for me to say that. I always wanted to be a comic book artist, but I was like, "Well, I don't draw like Jim Lee," or "I don't draw like Frank Miller." Right? No, you need to actually learn how to draw like John Jennings. You know what I'm saying? That's the thing. And so once I picked it back up again I realized that you know what? The style is basically a system of decisions that you make. You know? So that's what it is. It's just you're making a system of decisions for a particular reason that is very personal to you, and it comes out as a form. You know? And so, the forms that I make, I make for particular reasons, and they're mine. They don't belong to Frank Miller. I might be influenced by Frank Miller or Dennis or Lynd Ward or whoever. But I remix those through the meaning that is John, and that's what comes out. I wish I could tell myself that. I'd be a better artist now.

RH: Wow. Wow, that's cool. That's cool. Listen, this has been exceptionally fun.
JJ: Yeah. We should do it more.

RH: And you know we'll do it again. This is the beginning. I just want to thank you again, man, for making the time.
JJ: Oh, yeah. Thank you.

RH: And we're done. This show is brought to you by the University of California, Riverside. I'm your host Rickerby Hines. Thank you for joining us in the Creator State. Man, why did we decide to do this?
JJ: I don't know. I don't know why we decided to do anything. I mean, it's like again, I think that you come out with that particular predilection that your function is to be an artist.

RH: Yeah.
JJ: I would be doing what I'm doing anyway.

RH: Yes. Yeah.
JJ: I'm just fortunate to fall into a space where I can support myself and my life, and maybe buy a couple of comic books from time to time.

Conversations at the Cohen Center: Episode Two

BECCA EVANS / 2018

From the Cohen Center, November 27, 2018. https://jmucohencenter.podbean.com/e/episode-two-an-interview-with-john-jennings/. Reprinted with permission of The Cohen Center.

Becca Evans: Welcome to the Conversations at the Cohen Center. I'm Becca Evans and today I'm speaking with John Jennings, professor of media and cultural studies at the University of California at Riverside, award winning editor and artist. Welcome to our podcast.
John Jennings: Hello, thank you for having me.

BE: So let's just jump right in. Tell me a little bit about yourself and your work.
JJ: Ah man, where do I start? Currently I'm a professor of media and cultural studies at the University of California at Riverside. I teach classes around comics and contemporary culture. We just approved a minor in science fiction there, so I teach three courses in Afrofuturism. I'm currently teaching the comics' course and also an Afrofuturism and aesthetics course, which is an intro to black speculative culture, and in the winter I will be teaching a class on Afrofuturism and horror and one on comics because a lot of times comics isn't considered to be part of Afrofuturist, more of a cultural productive method but it always has been. So that's what I do as a teacher. But I'm a curator, artist, and editor, and I also make comics. For twenty years I taught as a graphic design professor. My background is in art, design history, design methodology, history, illustrations, and stuff like that.

BE: That's amazing. How did you know this is where you wanted to go for your career?
JJ: For the media pieces, you mean, or the comics or . . .

BE: Any of it.
JJ: I think that when you first start thinking about it, you don't think about it as a career. It's just a passion. You don't really know that much about it. Just for a little bit of background, I grew up in—I was born in 1970. And so I grew up in this kind of post–civil rights era of Mississippi in a very rural space. So we didn't have a lot of access to these more urbanized spaces when it came to comics and stuff. We weren't picking them up on the newsstands and stuff. We were getting them at Stop-N-Gos and gas stations. So you were kind of distant from how comics were made. But I knew early on that I wanted to do something connected to comics, right? I gave up on that dream and eventually became a commercial artist. But I guess the timing was perfect for me because when I was in graduate school *Understanding Comics* came out, the Scott McCloud book. So that really changed the way I looked at how I was making comics and how I was thinking about them as a medium. I was thinking maybe in the early nineties there was something to this. And so when I went back to teaching at the University of Illinois, at Urbana-Champagne, my love of hip-hop culture and comics began to rise to the surface, and I started to change how I thought about my scholarship. Maybe in the early 2000s or so is when I thought this is a career path with some validity.

BE: What was it like for you getting into academia, your MFA program?
JJ: It was difficult at first. Here's the thing, Jackson State is an HBCU. I studied commercial art, which is like the great-great-granddaddy of graphic design, and we weren't really well funded. So I didn't really understand what visual communication was. I was really trained as a fine artist. But the graphic communication stuff we had was like sign painting. It was very analog, and computers were just now peaking in. So we're talking the early nineties with the Macintoshes, where, oh by the way, you can make graphics, that type of thing. It changed everything, little did we know how much it was going to change everything. It was difficult for me because I was trying to figure out what graphic design was. I took three tries to get in the MFA program. I have a masters in arts degree and art education. And when I was at UCI I took undergraduate courses out of sequence to learn more about graphic design. The last time my mentor Tom Kovacs, God rest him, said, "Hey, why don't you send in a portfolio instead of sending just slides?" I put in a portfolio where they could see improvement. And that's when they said, "Okay, let's give this guy a shot." Once I got into the MFA program I was hungry. I did well, and eventually they hired me back to teach. I was the first African American chair of graphic design there. I was the second African American to receive tenure in

art in the school there. The current chair I help mentor, and two of my former students teach there.

BE: That's great.
JJ: I know; that's crazy, right?

BE: Are you, did you regret that it took you three tries, or do you think it helped you?
JJ: I think it helped me. One of the things that helps motivate me is when people tell me I can't do something. "Oh really, I'm going to show you." [laughs]

BE: Spite and pettiness.
JJ: Right. Oh my God, I'm the king of pettiness. I'm the mayor of petticoat junction; it's crazy.

BE: Sometimes you have to be in academia.
JJ: Well yes. And who are you to say what my limitations are? And I think they didn't realize how inherently judgmental and discriminatory their practices were. A lot of my work involves race and representation, so there are a lot of racialized micro-aggressions, particularly in that school. I used to call University of Illinois "upsouth." because basically there's certain vibes and energies that you're familiar with growing up in the Deep South. Overtly racist in some ways. And then you go to a space where you think it's not, and you know, yeah, that was kind of a racist statement; you just didn't know it. It's really interesting. Later on they did this whole study of racialized micro-aggressions out of that school. Interesting findings actually. So yes, there was some prejudgment of my abilities that I think they learned from later, and the professors that thought I couldn't work in that space became friends and strong mentors later.

BE: Could you talk about how you're identifying your work in today's society and what you're doing in the industry? Because you've talked about race and that's obviously a huge issue for you.
JJ: It's something I'm trying to un-design. I think fairly recently I came across speculative design. Speculative design is popularized by [Anthony] Dunne and [Fiona] Raby. They're this team out of the UK, and they do a lot of work around speculative narratives as ways to create objects or projects deliverable that become index for social issues. But they use science-fiction narratives to make these things. So I was thinking, first of all, they don't really deal

with Afrofuturist work like [Octavia] Butler's work, Nalo Hopkinson, Nnedi Okorafor, and all these science-fiction writers from the African diaspora or of African descent. And the other thing they don't think about in a broader context is the writing of people like, say, Derrick Bell, who is a science-fiction writer and happens to be one of the forefathers of critical race theory. There's got to be some connections there. So I started thinking as a fictionalized narrative. When I started teaching at the University of Buffalo there was this course called Race as Science Fiction because that's pretty much what it is. It's a fallacy that our identity is connected to this made up thing. There's a biological phenotype because of where your ancestors were from, because of the climate, the amount of sun you were getting. On a genetic level we are the same species. There's no difference. It's kind of like the optics of diversity. I just recently got my DNA ancestry and I'm 39 percent European, but the rest is mostly West African where my ancestors were snatched from. So I've been thinking about race as design and have been thinking about this idea of race as design study where thinking about the culpability of design in actually pushing particular notions about what race is and how it functions. What I've been doing is creating science-fiction narratives, comics, and social events to try to unmake that, to try to figure out how to either redesign that concept or just totally say, "Okay, here's proof that it doesn't matter." And I think stories can actually create intersections or empathy. That's what we need; we need to see the commonalities. I guess it's a human thing where you just see the differences and not the commonalities. So I want to try to design stories that make us see the commonalities.

BE: You've mentioned Afrofuturism a lot, which is an amazing concept. How do you define it?

JJ: I would say that Afrofuturism is a cultural production method, primarily narrative, that deals with speculative cultural production that is Afrocentric but is centralized around blackness or other perspectives that come out of the African diaspora. For me, and some people would argue about this, that the original Mark Dery definition talks about being African American but of late there's been a lot of speculative fiction and fantasy coming out of the continent, out of Africa and also coming from the diaspora from the islands, the Caribbean. In fact, Nalo Hopkinson, one of the premier science-fiction writers of that space, is Jamaican-Toronto, writes, like, Caribbean cyberpunk or Caribbean queer cyberpunk. Speculative fiction of the African diaspora perspective. And it's not just science-fiction stories, but dance, art, comics, plays. It goes into different production areas.

BE: What voices do you draw inspiration from, or do you draw inspiration from those in that community?
JJ: Even though they didn't know it, Milestone Media was part of that movement. Denys Cowan, Michael Davis, Dwayne McDuffie, God rest him. People in the black independent comics community are thriving. Writers like Samuel Delaney, Nalo Hopkinson, Nnedi Okorafor. Even Afro-Latino writers, too, like Daniel Jose Older, Tananarive Due. Visually I'm looking at people like Mishindu Kanumba, Mindy [inaudible], Sanford Biggers. Oh, more recently people like Jordan Peele, Ryan Coogler from *Black Panther*, Reynaldo Anderson, who's one of the premier scholars. Ytasha Womack, who's a reporter/journalist/author/therapist/dance artist. There's a lot, but mostly I draw from ancestral spaces. I want to know more about the culture and cultural practices that I want to try to inform the writing and creating that I make from.

BE: What other industry folks do you connect with to do the kind of work that you're doing? What fields do you branch out into? Who do you interact with?
JJ: Fairly recently I've been doing a lot of stuff in publishing. I'm really connected to the comics' community, multiple versions of it. A lot of people think that it's all one industry, but it's multi-formed just like most industries. The mainstream comic industry, which is direct market, I have connections there. I have strong connections with people like David Walker; Brian Michael Bendis; Ronald Wimberly, who's doing stuff with Image Comics; Sanford Greene; Chuck Browne. And also I have a book out with Lionforge, which is a black-owned comic-book company out of St. Louis. We have a book called *Black Comix Returns*, which is a collection of a hundred or so [independent artists]. In mainstream publishing our book *Kindred* is with Abrams publishing. So I have really strong connections with the Abrams ComicArt family there, publishers, editors. Just recently I was given my own imprint with them, a comics' publishing imprint. So we're going to be looking at primarily diverse, speculative fiction, across the board. And also some historic nonfiction. Mostly publishing. I have a pretty high profile in the academy too. I have a lot of friends and colleagues in the academy. So that's my main track, the academy and trade publishing.

BE: From your own projects *Blue Hand Mojo* to the graphic novel adaptation *Kindred* of Octavia Butler's novel, what's your favorite type of project to work on and why?
JJ: Well honestly, I would rather work on my own stuff. I'm really grateful and honored to have worked on *Kindred* and to work on the following books *Parable of the Sower* and *Parable of the Talents* back to back as well. If I had my

druthers I would work on my own stories because I have a gazillion stories, which is probably why I got an imprint. So it's like, how do we get these ideas out? But my favorite stories are the ones that come out from me and my collaborators. *Kindred* was an honor to do. It was a wonderful opportunity that I think has opened a lot of doors for us.

BE: Where do you draw inspiration from for those personal stories and where do you draw the inspiration to do this kind of work from?
JJ: I draw it from the future. I'm approaching fifty. I'll be forty-eight in November. I think that once you get to a certain age the death urge kind of kicks in. You realize that the likelihood of me living to be a hundred would be . . . who knows? You start thinking about your legacy and you start thinking about the things you want to leave behind, and for future generations, you know, if we don't drown ourselves with the polar icecaps melting. [laughs] We're in a weird space right now; it's kind of freaky. I don't know. I think I want to leave whatever I've learned in the past forty-eight years behind for people to learn and not make the same kind of mistakes that I have or make better mistakes. For the future, whatever future that might be.

BE: I like that. "Make better mistakes."
JJ: Yeah, fail safely.

BE: How do you see your art impacting the world?
JJ: Oh, I don't know. They need to tell me. I mean there's people who are fans of the work or are inspired by the work and they pop up on Facebook or on Instagram. I don't really think about it that much. I just have to do the best that I can with the time that I have. Hopefully, people are paying attention, but if they don't then I'm still going to make it. So I don't concern myself with the impact as much as I've got to get the stories out because the stories they don't let me alone. The images don't let me alone. I've got a million pictures and ideas; it's insane. And I try to work as hard as I can to get as much stuff out or take copious notes. Just in case—ah, well, he's not here anymore; maybe we can carry it on if we like the ideas. But I've been really good at pitching ideas to people so I collaborate a lot. I've found that most people don't have a lot of ideas. I know that's kind of weird to say. They may have one really good idea and some okay ideas. I get haunted by amazing notions. Like wouldn't it be great if we did this thing or this show or this idea or logo, and I have to figure out ways to get them done. So I pitch them to people, and if they like them we work on it together. I share the IP because I'm not like Disney. I don't have

millions of dollars. But we do have control over the intellectual property. That is how that works. Me and my friend Stacey [Robinson] started this loosely collective called Motherboxx Studios, which came out of the *Kindred* project because that's where I learned I can't do everything by myself. We had a small amount of time to do that book, and I pinched a nerve working on the book. And I needed help. I figured out how to use help. I think that actually created a more studio vibe. Now when I think about projects I think about teams.

BE: It sounds like collaboration is a huge piece of what you do.
JJ: Yes, it is. I love it. It's necessary, I think, to get things done. And when you share ideas you make them stronger. Because when you share an idea it's like what about this, and what do you think about this? They're poking holes in it, or they're filling in the holes themselves. Especially if you have someone that has a really quick story mind, and you're going back forth. Well, what if this character has red hair instead of blue hair? How would that change the story? Stories are experiments, but they're also problem-solving devices to me. You're writing about a particular thing. What is a problem you're trying to solve? To me it's all design. A product or deliverable is just a system of decisions or story-making turns to get to a particular thing. We always think about the end result, but everything has a story connected to it. And some of them are sad, and some of them are scary. You don't really think about what the story of that thing is.

BE: So what are your favorite types of stories to tell?
JJ: Horror stories.

BE: Really?
JJ: Yeah, I'm a big horror fan. Because here's the thing, when you're scared you're either going to do two things: you're either going to run from the thing that scares you or you're going to fight the thing that scares you. It's a fight or flight response. You may wonder how the hell to get up out of there. You know what I'm saying. Just to protect yourself. Well, what if you can't; what are the decisions? I think that when you're terrified there's pretty much pure that's who you are primally. Those decisions you have to make in that particular time. Those are the times when you become either the villain or the hero or the coward or whatever you're going to be. The other thing is that a lot of decision making is made from fear. Not from love unfortunately. People say that love makes the world go round. That's very nice and that looks good on a Valentine's day card, but really I think it's about the stuff we really are afraid of, the things

we don't understand, and we create laws and regulation and walls and different things to actually deal with the things that freak us out. When you deal with the other there are three things that you're going to do. Either you're going to try to assimilate the other, destroy the other, or separate yourself from them. That's human nature; that's what we've always done. And those are all fear related. If you don't understand something you really are like undercutting it or creating narratives around it to justify how we treat that thing. And those are all horror stories. You know if you go out there those people down the street are bad news; you know they could chop you up and eat you. You know, is that true? [laughs]You know what I'm saying? My mom was a huge horror fan, action movie fan. So I grew up on a steady diet of exploitation films, horror films, [Alfred] Hitchcock films, Edgar Allan Poe. I grew up in the South, in the woods. So I had this really active imagination early on. And I think as a technology horror is very useful to unpack social injustice issues. For instance if you look at all the *Twilight Zone* stuff or *Tales from the Crypt*, they're all like morality tales. They're talking about what it means to be human, what the decisions you make mean at a particular situation. Weird fiction and horror are my favorite things because it's hard to scare the hell out of people. We've seen so many things especially with comics. It's really very difficult to make a scary comic. Comics like Gail Simone's *Arcane Room*—she's one of my favorite writers. I hope she hears this. Or like Becky Cloonan's *Southern Cross*. That's a good book; that's a really good book. In fact, I want more of it. So I want to write more like that. [And have people say,] "This is unsettling. What's next?" Because it prepares us for these fights we have to have. These existential dregs. The sticky, nasty part of being human. It's not all sunshine. I think I've always had an affinity for those kinds of stories. Someone has to write them. I make fun stuff too like *Kid Code*, this crazy time-travel, hip hop, graffiti-inspired thing; it's nuts. But mostly I write, I have an affinity for dealing with darker subjects without having them affect me as much as other people. Maybe it's because my mom and I talked about what would scare us. We'd watch horror movies together and talk about why that was scary. We'd have conversations, and she'd say, "I saw that you were shaking. What was that about?" So we'd have these conversations about horror and what's scary. And it's made it apparent to me that is a mechanism that you can talk about these issues with. I teach a whole class on Afrofuturism and horror.

BE: I would love to take that class.
JJ: And when I was at UB [University of Buffalo] I taught an art class Media Is the Monster. So it's all about monster as a mechanism to talk about the other.

UNIVERSITY
OF SOUTH CAROLINA
AFRICAN
AMERICAN
STUDIES
Est. 1971

UNIVERSITY
OF SOUTH CAROLINA
AFRICAN
AMERICAN
STUDIES
Est. 1971

An example of graphic design, from the University of South Carolina African American Studies. © 2019 John Jennings, permission of John Jennings.

We had a whole section on the demonization of female sexuality. I might have traumatized some of those students because I was showing them some wild stuff. But we had to make an art show afterwards, and I think overall people liked the class. It's funny; we would have this one young lady who would laugh when she was scared at the most terrifying moments. She would apologize and say, "I'm sorry. I was so scared." I was like, "You're ruining the movie."

BE: You've talked about your students a lot. What advice do you give them when they ask how they can do what you do?

JJ: First of all, don't try this at home. But it would be follow your bliss. I know that's very Joseph Campbell, but the decisions I've made have been led by that little voice in my chest, in my head, in my soul that doesn't feel right; you're on the wrong path. You should go this way because that's the thing you're attracted to. I think as I've gotten older, I've gotten better at that. I've gotten better at my instincts and what feels right to me. If you really know yourself, if you pay attention to yourself, you'll do what you need to be doing. If you want to be an artist, be an artist because life is short and nothing is promised. Everything is like on the edge. Anything can happen. If you're going to go out, go out doing what you love. And if you don't want to be a doctor, don't be one. Forget what your parents say. They don't know everything. They don't. Yes, they brought you into the world, they fed you, but guess what? You're your own person, and you have to be happy with the decisions that you make. With my students I'm like, "Play hard and learn from your mistakes." But really pay attention to the mistakes you make because they teach you things too. So those are the things that I talk about. They'll be afraid to ask questions and to live a life. And I think the more you live your life the more you understand yourself and others. And the more you understand others you'll figure out where you need to be. Because college is just the beginning. [If a student says,] "You didn't give me what I needed." Oh yes, I did. I gave you exactly what you needed. You'll know that maybe a decade later. Thank you. Congratulations. You're now a human being. Go out into the world and be bold. I think again that's fear. You're afraid to fail. Honestly, when I graduated from high school I was seventeen and I always wanted to be an artist, but I didn't have any road map. I had no road map and my mom, she encouraged me to be an artist, but she thought it was a hobby. When I said I wanted to be an artist, she was like, "What? No, I want you to . . ." I wasn't even living with my mom at the time, I was living with my grandparents, but I still listened to her as counsel because she was my mom. [She said,] "Well, I'd rather you be a doctor or a lawyer or retire from the military, anything but that. You're going to die in a box, cut off your ear, just some crazy stuff. [Laughing] She had no conception; no one knew that art is an actual profession that you could have and be successful. Somebody's making all this stuff. But we didn't know. If you can't see it, you can't be it. So I've always endeavored to become the type of teacher that I always needed. I wanted to become the person that I needed when I was young. So when someone like myself comes across me I'm like, "Yes, I see." I can do this, create a path. Let's make it easier for future generations, so you can track my path. Oh this dude did these things. The other thing is I did go to the military actually, but I was running away from who I was. I ran to the military to run away from becoming an artist. But I hurt myself in an accident and have a piece of steel in my right foot. And that's when I realized parents don't know everything. My mom was wrong; she was really wrong. And I was like, "You know what? I don't know what the hell is going to happen, but I need to be an artist." And the universe itself, God the creator, you know Santa Claus—whatever you want to call it—every spirit out there was like, "Dude, you're on the wrong path. So we're going to literally break your foot to show you symbolically that you're on the wrong path." So I went to Jackson State for art. I didn't know what the hell I was going to do, but I made a life out of art. And I did what was right for me. So that's what I try to teach the students. Don't try to be like me; try to be like you. But first you have to figure out what the hell that is. Get through the rigmarole of being a human being. What feeds me and what feeds my soul. At the end of the day, when you look back at it do you want regrets? Or do you want to be like, "You know, I was on a rollercoaster, and I had my arms up the whole time"?

BE: Take life as it hits you.
JJ: That's right exactly.

BE: Last question. If you went out tomorrow what would you consider to be your defining work that you'd want people to recognize after you're gone?
JJ: That's really tough. I don't know. I've done a lot of stuff, and I'm really proud of a lot of things. It's probably going to be in my students. Whatever legacy my students bring or the black comics' festival I co-created at the Schomburg. The kids that come through there, they don't have to go through what I went through. I think that's actually a cool legacy to leave behind. I theorized about a lot of things, I made some work, but I think for the most part conversations that I've had with spaces. Creating spaces where people can be empowered. Those are probably the proudest things because they're ongoing. So SOL-CON, the Black Comics' Art Festival on the West Coast, and the

The cover of *Sunspot Jungle: The Ever Expanding Universe of Fantasy and Science Fiction, Vol. I* (2018). © 2019 John Jennings, permission of Rosarium Publishing.

Harlem festival are part of my legacy. I'm really proud of that; they were very successful. They feed a lot of people, here, in their soul. That might be it, but I've taught thousands of students because I started teaching at twenty-seven. So, I've been in the trenches a long time.

BE: You've influenced a lot of people. That's a great thing.
JJ: Hopefully for the best. We'll see.

BE: Thank you so much for joining me on this podcast.
JJ: It was great talking to you.

Film Sense: Afrofuturism and the Ethno-Gothic

FRANK H. WOODWARD / 2019

From the Podcast Film Sense, April 28, 2019. http://filmsense.libsyn.com/film-sense-afro-futurism-ethno-gothic. Reprinted by permission of Frank H. Woodward.

Black Panther, *Get Out*, *Candyman* all have become classics of speculative fiction. They are also shining examples of Afrofuturism and the Ethno-Gothic. With the success of these films, it may seem that a new subgenre of fantastic cinema is being born. But according to Professor John Jennings, horror and science fiction have been depicting the black experience for quite some time. What we have instead is a renaissance. So join Professor Jennings and myself as we explore this new birth.

Frank H. Woodward: I'm here with Professor John Jennings at the University of California, Riverside.
John Jennings: Hello, how are you doing? Thank you for having me.

FHW: Thank you for coming on. John has two phrases that I got to know more about by seeing John speak. They are Afrofuturism and Ethno-Gothic. From my point of view they seem more like subgenres of the horror, science-fiction, and fantasy realms. But they've kind of been with us for a longer time than people think.
JJ: That's correct. The general term would be black speculative culture, but that's a mouthful. But they definitely have a genre component to it but also have these cultural-movements kinds of aspects to them as well. I would liken them to this generation's version of the Harlem Renaissance or even the Black Arts Movement where you see a lot of this creative speculative work that is being generated by primarily black or brown artists that are dealing directly with pop and political movements as well. I was looking at the fact that a lot of this newer-generation-speculative culture was being connected to or intersecting

with the movements of black lives. For instance, where this notion of speculation of the future is a contentious notion. And so yes, honestly, those are the things I started thinking about when Stanford Carpenter and I came up with the term "Ethno-Gothic" because Afrofuturism seemed to be this kind of cultural production space. And we're like, "Well, does, like, everything that is Afrocentric and speculative get couched under that, or do we ignore genre?" So that's what started me thinking about these things. For instance, do you put *Blade* under Afrofuturism, or is that horror? You know it has horror aspects, it has adventure spaces, and there's also a kind of sci-fi story. So what do you do with those different nuances?

FHW: In the post–*Black Panther* world it almost becomes a little easier because *Black Panther* is purely Afrofuturism in a lot of ways.
JJ: Right. It's definitely one of the reasons why there's a lot of the conversations about it because it's such a huge film, even though the character was created in 1966 and the term "Afrofuturism" was posited thirty-three years later in 1993. So we've definitely seen a resurgence in black popular culture that is centered around speculation, either science-fiction, fantasy, horror, magical realism, or what have you, and how it also intersects with political ideas with representation in particular.

FHW: Of course with the work of Jordan Peele, the most obvious example for a lot of people, that may be why a lot of people are interested more in these topics now that these two films have come out like juggernauts.
JJ: That and also *Into the Spiderverse*. You've also seen a resurgence in the interest in people of color being producers. You have the youngest executive producer in the history of Hollywood who is this young, black girl from *Blackish*. I forgot her name [Marsai Martin]. For the new movie *Little*, she's a producer on that. She actually has a deal with Universal now; she's fourteen. But this is a speculative story; it's a comedy. If you think about it, it's kind of like if you took *Big*, the Tom Hanks movie, and mixed it with *The Devil Wears Prada*, and that's what you've got. But it's a speculative story. It's about a wish. It has magic in it. So it's speculative stuff, totally a fantasy story.

FHW: Absolutely. We're going to delve into this episode folks, but before we do that we're going to get more of a background on John. Professor John Jennings, like I said, you are a professor here at the University of California, Riverside, in media and cultural studies. I first encountered you at the Horrible Imaginings Film Festival last year where you gave a panel discussion about

scary black folks: Race Studies in Horror, and that is what introduced me to the term "Ethno-Gothic," which I had not heard before.
JJ: That's because I made it up—me and my friend Stanford came up with that.

FHW: It's a great name. And also too, when you go back maybe we'll do a little of that today to just trace the history of what you consider Ethno-Gothic. You realize it has been with us longer than we think. But you're also an award-winning graphic novelist, editor, and festival organizer. Some of the books that you have out now are *Blue Hand Mojo*, *Black Kirby: In Search of the Motherboxx Connection*, and *Cosmic Underground: A Grimoire of Black Speculative Discontent*, and you won the Bram Stoker Award for Octavia Butler's *Kindred*. And I understand you are also working on an adaptation on another one of her stories.
JJ: Yes, Damian Duffy, who is my co-adapter, and I, we're doing the *Parable* duology. So we're doing *Parable of the Talents* and *Sower*. We're doing *Parable of the Sower* first. It's actually set in Southern California. It's kind of like a dystopian, Afrofuturist, feminist story. It's really kind of scary because it's so prescient. It's about a young lady from the IE; I guess she is from around this area or close to LA. And there's a populous president that takes over who wants to make America great again. This was written in the late eighties as I recall. She [Butler] was referring to [Ronald] Reagan at the time. So the whole infrastructure of the country is falling apart, and there's wildfires everywhere. It's tomorrow is what it is. So it's been very harrowing to work on this book. It's two parts, and the main character ends up founding her own religion. You should really check it out; it's one of her best books.

FHW: Folks should check it out as well and also keep an eye out for the graphic novel when it comes out.
JJ: It's coming out in January 2020.

FHW: You also are behind some media installations and museum exhibits, and that was one of the things I was introduced to in your classes that you also teach here. You just had an exhibit here in Riverside called *Uncaged*, and it was about the impact of the Marvel hero Luke Cage. And going through there, there was one of the cards that really struck me, and it was titled Racism as Science Fiction. And that phrase was like, "Whoa." Can you explain more by what you mean by how racism is science fiction?
JJ: Race as Science Fiction. The title comes from a class when I taught at the University of Buffalo. I actually taught a full blown Afrofuturist graphic

novel studio, I mean, graphic design studio. I used to teach a class called Applied Semiotics there, and essentially it was an introduction to semiotics for graphic design artists and for vision communicators. What I would do is I would change the theme every year. So for instance the first theme was like space and identity. And so all the projects dealt with how do we utilize space to talk about who we are? I did one called the Media Is the Monster. That's where I started thinking about these things in a very practical way. I subjected the students to a ton of horror movies, and we talked about the idea of the grotesque as a way to talk about otherness and political dichotomies of the monster. And then the last class I did within that space was an Afrofuturistic graphic design studio where they were exposed to works by Samuel Delaney and Nalo Hopkinson and Nnedi Okorafor, all these big science-fiction and fantasy writers who happen to be people of color, and started thinking about the idea that race has two components to it. One is the falsehood that we are really different biologically. We are the same species; we are the same people. The other component is socially constructed, and that social construction is just a narrative. So it is like science fiction—well, this person is like this because this one component of their physical makeup. And that's totally false. What happens is we take these phenotypical differences that are more about where our ancestors came from than it is about anything else. Well, my hair is different because it was hotter, and my ancestors' hair would protect me from the sun—you know, that type of thing. That's the only thing, right? And other than that it's really stories about how we are supposed to function as people from different "races." This is like a science-fiction story, so it's race as science fiction. How do you unpack those fictions, and how do you create other types of narratives that actually push back against those falsehoods?

FHW: And with race, tying into the fear of the other is definitely something that the horror genre has always tapped into.
JJ: Very much so.

FHW: Sticking with Luke Cage for a second, that's also true. This very strong, indestructible black man is the biggest threat, I think, to white superiority more than anything. And it's a total fiction on their part.
JJ: That's right, exactly. And so the notion of stereotypes is, like, stereotypes are constructed by the people who are in control of the production of them. And then the people who are being stereotyped are forced to live inside those stereotypes. They're projected upon us. They're almost like prisons. And when you think about how the word "stereotype" is connected, first of all it comes

out of the printing tradition; it's a printing term. It was created in the 1800s by this French gentleman named Firmin Didot, just like the typeface. He'd come from a long line of printers and paper makers. Stereotype basically was when you needed to print like one sheet over and over again so they would use papier-mâché and make a cast, and they would print it over and over again. And it was called stereotype. We don't start to use it the way we talk about it until the 1920s when this gentleman named Walter Lippmann, who was a newspaper man who started to re-appropriate the idea of stereotype. The root word of stereotype is stereo, which is a Greek word that means hard or fixed. So, if you think about it stereotype is really about fixity. So when you see someone you're judging them; you're fixing them in a particular way. You're saying this is who you are. And what happens is the generalizations of a stereotype become the thing that represents an entire subgroup of people. And then what happens is you start making these assumptions and creating those fictions and narratives about them. And then in particular if you have an amount of power you start to affect policies and laws, telling people where they can and cannot live. You see this is when it becomes a really big issue. When people talk about the idea of "I'm not a racist person," or that particular person has been taken care of, they're not thinking about the system. Racism is a system, or, how we divide each other up as a system. And so stereotypes are just the beginning. You get rid of all the stereotypes you'll still have this kind of system or multiple systems that these things are based on.

FHW: Which is something I think people are coming to terms with—that we're trying to get rid of the stereotypes and get rid of all the glasses that make us look at each other differently. There are those that don't realize that there's an institutional bias and bigotry that's there.
JJ: That is actually in the foundation of the creation of the institution. That's the thing. It's really difficult. And institutions are really good at not changing. That's their superpower actually. [laughs] They're like, "Watch me not change. I'm just going to stay here.' And so what you try to do is you utilize narratives to interrogate or critique those resistant structures.

FHW: So is that where Afrofuturism started to come into being. If I remember correctly the person who coined the phrase was Mark Dery in 1993.
JJ: When Dery is positing Afrofuturism he's looking at a system of narratives because a lot of our black sci-fi is actually in music. You think about Lisa Kratz-Perry's work or Parliament Funkadelic or Sun Ra's work, they're all science-fiction stories. They just happen to be auditory in their sci-fi stories.

Or even people like the work of Deltron 3030 or even the Detroit techno movement or people like Underground Resistance, they have an entire narrative connected to science fiction and their stories. There's a really great book on the subject that I just happen to have right here, which is *More Brilliant than the Sun: Adventures in Sonic Fiction* by Kodwo Eshun, and it happens to be one of the seminal books on Afrofuturism because it starts to analyze music as sci-fi narrative.

FHW: We're going to be posting a few links to different books and stuff.
JJ: I have a whole list of stuff I can send you because I've been teaching this for the last few years. I'm going to get back to your query, but what's really interesting to me about this particular cultural movement is that if you look at a lot of cultural production spaces that deal with popular culture, the academy that is people like myself who are teaching in colleges and universities; we're chasing the pop-cultural event usually. Usually, we're like, "Wait. What's this thing? Let's go after it. Oh, let's go look at punk music," you know that type of thing. Very seldom do you see academics pushing the envelope. If you look at something like hip hop it took us a while to catch up. It took us a long time to catch up with this phenomenon making billions of dollars before people started studying it. Afrofuturism and black speculative culture, I was part of a vanguard of black scholars and cultural scholars who were studying this for, like, a decade before *Black Panther* jumped off, before Jordan Peele was making his films. It was interesting to see that something that doesn't happen a lot when you look at how cultural spaces are formed. But back to your thing about Dery he was looking at those particular spaces. His article on Afrofuturism where he posits the term—he's looking at music and also looking at science -fiction and fantasy writers like Samuel R. Delaney, Nalo Hopkinson. He interviews Delaney, and he interviews Greg Tate, who's a leading African American cultural scholar, musician, and just a renaissance man who is one of the most brilliant cultural scholars to probably come out of the academy, even off the street. This brother's dope. And also he [Dery] talked to Tricia Rose, who at the time was either [working on or] writing *Black Noise*, which is the first really, really earliest serious of books about hip-hop culture. Those are the main three. But basically they were saying that there weren't a lot of black science-fiction writers at the time that you knew about. But if you knew you could expand about how you know about black speculative culture, then you get a lot more though. And that's why Sheree Renee Thomas's book is so important. Her first collection *Dark Matter: A Century of Speculative Fiction from the African Diaspora*, which I want to say as a publication came out in the 1990s

or the early 2000s, one or the other. Basically what she posits is that the stuff that we're looking at—works by Delaney or W. E. B. Du Bois or Countee Cullen or Zora Neale Hurston—can also be considered speculative because they're using these kinds of imaginary, magical realist tendencies to talk about social issues. So those can also be considered science-fiction and fantasy stories. And so when you start thinking about it that way you start to expand your canon to what we've been doing for over a hundred years. It pushes back against the tropes of traditional European genre and opens up the conversation a lot. I'm thinking of this particular version of what we're seeing is simply the arc coming back around. These are the same types of stories we've always been telling.

FHW: In that notion of it always being there is what also struck me about your Ethno-Gothic speech that you gave at the festival about how black horror, or at least the black experience in horror films, has been with us for some time.
JJ: That's right. Meanwhile, Frances Stanford Carpenter, who's a cultural anthropologist, we were hanging out and talking about being excited about seeing what is happening in black sci-fi. And this had to be a few years ago, maybe in 2010, 2011, and we started thinking, "Well, what about genre?" How does something like *Kindred*, for instance, which is a speculative story by Octavia Butler about a black woman who is married to a white man—and this is in the late seventies, so this is a taboo. They're moving into their house near LA in Southern California. The book is written in 1979 but takes place in 1976, our country's bicentennial, and she did it on purpose to talk about the trapping of how race is constructed in America. So they're both writers; he's a little bit older, a little more successful. What ends up happening is they're unpacking boxes, and then all of a sudden right in front of the husband's eyes, his wife who happens to be black is teleported inexplicably back through time to the middle of a slave plantation. Now what's really interesting about this is that if you're reading the book you don't realize that Dana, which is the main character's name, is black until the N-word is dropped the second time she goes back. You don't even know she's black. So then it becomes a horror story. Then it becomes a horror story, and you're like, "What!?!" So of course we didn't have that power in a comic book because the character is the character. You couldn't do it because it's the affordance of the medium. So there's not a TARDIS or a DeLorean or any kind of time travel H. G. Wellian mechanism that is employed here. It's some kind of existential, supernatural force that is pulling her back through time. She starts to realize that when she gets there—the first time she gets there she ends up on a bank of a river, and she sees this little white kid with red hair drowning. His name is Rufus;

we find that out later. She instinctively jumps into the water and saves him, gives him CPR. Then his mother is freaking out because she has really short hair, and she's dressed—she has on bell-bottoms and stuff. To her she looks like a man and thinks that this man is attacking her son. And then she [Dana] hears this click of a gun being cocked and turns around, and there's a shotgun in her face. And that's Rufus' father. So then she instantly is teleported back home to 1976 and on the other side of the room, and it's only like a few seconds later. And her husband is like, "What just happened? You're wet; you're muddy. What is going on?" And little by little she realizes that this little white kid is her great-great-great grandfather. And every time he's in trouble she's automatically pulled back to save his life. It's almost like this twisted back-to-the-future thing. And then little by little she starts to realize that not only is this the truth, that she has to save this dude in order for her to exist, she has to facilitate the torture and rape of her great-great-great grandmother in order for her to exist in her own time. It's a very painful thing. It's gothic right? So I'm saying, does this fit with Afrofuturism? Whose Afrofuture is this because you have the chronopolitics of the future and the definition of the Afrofuture? So how does Afrofuturism deal with time differently and narrative differently? These are the things we're looking at. You can either say: well Afrofuturism deals with time differently and then couch everything under it, or you could say are there other subgenres under black speculative culture and that Afrofuturism is just one of those things. And that's when we came up with the idea of the Ethno-Gothic. The idea that we came up with—well, what about dealing with the ideals of trauma around racial difference or around racial pain that we actually have in our country—and then creating narratives to unpack those traumas. I don't know if you're familiar with the Erykah Badu song "Bag Lady"? It's about this bag lady who's dragging all this stuff behind her trying to catch a bus, and she's saying you need to pack light, you need to drop those bags so that you could get on that bus to the future. So to me the Ethno-Gothic is a way to unpack those bags so you could get on that bus to the Afrofuture. So I think that's the connection, because we're going to carry all these horrible, traumatic things that have happened to us, not only black people in America but Americans. People don't understand that when you hurt someone, when you're systemically hurting someone you're undoing your own soul too. It's not just you, it's a double trauma, and you're going to reap the benefits of that too. Of course if you start looking at epigenetic trauma and how trauma and pain is passed through our DNA, then you need to understand, you need to deal with those ghosts. And so the Ethno-Gothic uses gothic tropes like the ghosts, the haunted house, the doppelganger, haunted artifacts to deal with those traumas.

FHW: And so as we mentioned earlier Jordan Peele has definitely tapped into that with the doppelganger with *Us*.
JJ: *Us* is definitely what I'm thinking. When I think about the Ethno-Gothic those are both primary things because you're also looking at issues around otherness and also isolation and imprisonment, the creation of the other through space. You know the sunken place to me is a metaphor for race and space, the conflation of race and space in general. That's the bad side of town, or that's the opposite side of the tracks. That's the same kind of notion of don't go over there, that's where those people are, that's the sunken place.

FHW: Another film that you've mentioned that you feel has connections to this—an obvious choice now that we think about it—is *Candyman*. How does *Candyman* line up with the gothic for those who don't want to do the work for themselves?
JJ: Well, here's the thing—*Candyman*, well first of all, the film takes an actual event that happened in Chicago and marries it with the story *The Forbidden* by Clive Barker. It talks about the oral history of trauma. So this character Candyman is a painter named Daniel Robitaille, who's the son of a man who creates a mechanism for creating different types of shoes or something; he's a wealthy black man. And what happens is he's hired by this wealthy landowner to paint an image of his beautiful daughter. They fall in love with each other, she's impregnated, and they have a child. We see that in the second movie. What happens essentially is that Candyman is lynched by a lynch mob, he's stung to death by bees, and honey is smeared all over his body. His hand that he would create art with is taken from him and replaced with a hook. Then he becomes this spook story. He's like the king of all urban legends. So you marry together three different urban legends: the hook man with the hook hand, Bloody Mary, and race because remember race doesn't exist. It doesn't exist; it's a spook story. So when you start marrying those things together you get those really interesting, very, very smart critiques of black spaces. Because when you look at the film, you see Cabrini Green. Cabrini Green is a scary space. They've just finished talking about all the shootings that happened in Chicago today not realizing that Englewood is only one small part of a massive city. They make it seem like Chicago is a town. It's the third largest city in the country. Cabrini Green also doesn't exist anymore, it's now a ghost. The high rises that those films take place in were torn down.

FHW: I came from Philadelphia, the projects in Philly were not as scary as Cabrini Green, but they were a scary place.

JJ: But here's the thing, what creates the structure of the other? Those particular places were set up there to separate people. When you look at Chicago, when you look at the federally supported practice of redlining when people migrated up from the South, they couldn't live anywhere else but in the south side of Chicago, which was called Bronzeville. They called it Bronzeville because everybody there was bronze. My wife's from Chicago, so we know this history very well. And I'm from Mississippi originally, and a lot of my folk hit up 55 and went to Chicago and Detroit. So, anyway, Candyman migrates up from there too. I love the idea of him being an oral history piece. And to circle back to Luke Cage it's the same thing with him. He's from the South, and he's painted as this black boogey man. These particular stories are created to codify blackness and otherness in a particular way, it always has been, and that's what *Candyman* starts to explore.

FHW: And characters like Luke Cage, now that you've brought him up again, and Black Panther just because comic book characters in general evolve with their times and can be a reflection of things. One of the things from the Luke Cage exhibit was about having a character like Luke Cage, a bulletproof black man in a hoodie in today's world.

JJ: Yes. You have to know Cheo Hodari Coker; when he was creating that [television] series he was thinking about that a lot, particularly in the second series when he starts to push the envelope a lot around the intersections between history and science. For instance the character Bushmaster, who's getting his powers from Obeah which is a Jamaican mystical tradition, is very similar to something like hoodoo or conjure culture. So one of the things I'm really into is how do you take these old sciences and mix them with these new sciences. Essentially, Luke Cage, he's also an index to talk about the prison industrial complex. He's also an index to talk about medical apartheid. All these things are happening, and then *Candyman* also has these similar things where you're looking at the demonization of black, male sexuality and black male power and jealousy too. He was an erudite, a very well-educated black man who had a particular skillset, and he's wealthy. How dare he be the thing you said he was? And so what he does is he becomes a thing that is projected of the stereotype of the scary black man. And the hook of course, the phallic tendencies of a hook, my God, you're literally puncturing people's bodies and ripping their insides out. It's obvious that this is a psychosexual construction as well. Sorry I just went off on a tangent.

FHW: No, those are the tangents I want you to go off on. I think that's what's interesting about any genre, we always hear the expression that all stories have been told, and it's how you tell them. These two genres are how you tell them in a lot of ways, taking that point of view, that experience, that history and applying them to the gothic or what have you.
JJ: Right, or the sci-fi or the fantasy. Look at N. K. Jemison's work. She's won three consecutive Hugo Awards for best novel for her fantasy series. That's amazing, but it just goes to show that these other perspectives are valid. People want to see them. People want to hear about these things. People are tired of the same old thing. Don't get me wrong. I love me some Sherlock Holmes and King Arthur and Daredevil. I love all that stuff. But I also love these newer things that are coming from other cultural perspectives because, guess what, we all live here and all of our stories are valid.

FHW: It gives the world of storytelling more life. Also there's been a cry for diversity in television shows for a while now, and now that's slowly coming to be. People are like, "Oh wow, look at all these new ideas," but people, their stories have been waiting to be told.
JJ: They've been waiting for so long. It's really ridiculous. One of the most exciting things I just saw is this comic book that I've worked on. And actually I showed pictures from it at the Harlem [inaudible] called *Bitter Root*, and it's by Chuck Brown, David Walker, and Sanford Greene. And essentially it's pure Ethno-Gothic when I think about it. You're fighting against hatred as a monster. So it's the manifestation of hate as an evil thing. I did the editing on the back matter. I would put together essays and the letters column each issue. And it just got picked up for development by Legendary Pictures. Also, the same day we get the announcement that HBO has greenlit a series based on the Asunder world, which is from Stranger Comics, an LA-based comic book company. One of the founders, Sebastian Jones, used to work in music and parlayed that into working in comics, and now one of the most successful comics that he did was with Amandla Stenberg, an actress from *The Hunger Games* and *The Hate U Give*. And this can turn into an HBO series. This isn't DC or Marvel; this is an independent comic book company out of LA that was kick-starting books. And now to have an HBO series, it's crazy. [laughs]

FHW: One of the questions I was going to ask you about is this name in futurism about looking into the future, how do you see things coming along in the next few years? But I think we're already talking about that. Now studios are getting open to these stories. More writers are either getting graphic novels or

independent films produced of their own stories. I think it's going to continue to grow, don't you?
JJ: I think so too. And the reason why I think so is because if something is profitable it grows. And I can see this black speculative cultural turn becoming mainstream or more something like hip hop, for instance. Hip hop was first, "Oh it's going to be a flash in the pan, but let's make our money." And now it's part of everything. I think what's going to happen, too, is that you have these different subgenres and cultural movements that just become a part of or be, like *Blacula*, but more Afrofuturist, and people would be like, "I get it." That's what's about to happen because of all these different development deals. For instance, you saw that Viola Davis has a development deal with Amazon. She just signed an Octavia Butler TV series called *Wildseed*, based on one of her most popular novels. It's going to be spearheaded by Wanuri Kahiu, who is a Kenyan writer-director, and Nnedi Okorafor, who is an amazing, world famous science fiction–fantasy award-winning writer. They're show writers for a new show based off of Octavia Butler's work on Amazon Prime. So yes, we're looking at a very interesting time when politically these things are lining up, and you have more people of color and more people who are open-minded spearheading these things. When you open up something like that you have to fill it.

FHW: I encourage filmmakers as they try to conceive of their films to maybe start looking at some of these fictions, these short stories just because there's an untapped wealth of narrative that is sitting there in the literary side of Afrofuturism that has yet to see the small or big screen.
JJ: That's correct, and there's an audience for these stories obviously. And that's why I think you can't say that black lit films don't do well. You can't say that anymore. You haven't been able to say that for a while actually. But now you really can't say that.

FHW: No you can't, people will look at you cross-eyed and tell you to stand over there.
JJ: It's not a flash in the pan. People emulate these actors, and they see something that's cool. I mean *Into the Spiderverse* was great; that was a great film.

FHW: The offerings that have been coming out in cinema lately and on television too, some of the anthology shows that have been on, it's fresh, it's interesting, and it's well worth looking into. And if you're a producer looking into these things and finding these talents to give a voice to it is even more worth it. I think it would give the art form more longevity. The only thing that annoys

me a little bit is that for women and people of color they're finally getting their time up at the plate and at a time when the business is changing so radically. So everybody's getting a chance now to finally make these films when making a film from a business side of view is a little bit more complicated and confusing than it ever has been. But the thing that's encouraging is where people have heard on this podcast before is that I've been in pitch meeting after pitch meeting where *Get Out* is this new standard. They call it smart horror, but what it is is elevated horror that's talking about topics—well, it's doing what it should be. For me science fiction and horror were always westerns in the sense that westerns were about good versus evil for a while. But after a while they started hanging everything from racism to nationalism to sexism. These westerns were about some sort of cultural topic, and science fiction and horror do well with that.
JJ: Yes they do. That's because they speak so metaphorically and allegorically. That's why *Us* works so well. Don't worry about where they got the red suits. If you start looking at it like that it doesn't seem like it's making any sense. But if you take if from the allegory about otherness and about class and about nationhood, then it becomes a brilliant film.

FHW: We know that he's always been a very talented guy [Jordan Peele].But the fact that he's been sitting on these really in-depth stories that he just pulled out of the air. It's amazing. That means he's got a catalog someplace.
JJ: He's a very serious, very thoughtful man. I had a chance to sit with him for a while at his place and talk to him about *Get Out* and some other things, the Ethno-Gothic because I based my class off of *Get Out*. I just couldn't teach it because I was still at Harvard doing this fellowship. So I had this class, but I was at another school. I hadn't even moved here yet because I wrote the class the same day I saw *Get Out*. I couldn't stop thinking about it. I went back to my office and banged out a syllabus in like two hours. It was really easy to write because I had already been teaching in that era, so when I came here it was one of the first classes I wanted to do. And it has been very successful. I think where students really engage with it well is my Afrofuturism and Visual Culture of Horror class because of the fact that this stuff resonates so well. And it totally makes sense when you see the allegory buried in a lot of the work. He's a very powerful person. He's very much a horror fan, extremely humble as well. And I'm looking forward to seeing the other work that he does.

FHW: Absolutely. You're a teacher of pop culture, but you also consider yourself, like myself, a mega-geek.
JJ: Yeah, I'm a mega-geek. I'm a professional geek like yourself.

FHW: It was funny because I thought to myself, Do I wear my Frankenstein shirt today?
JJ: Look what I have on . . . I got this at Wonder-Con.

FHW: But you have a very interesting background because your mother was a teacher of literature.
JJ: No, she studied—she ended up going to Alcorn State University in literature. She didn't finish because of me. So she was doing odd jobs and stuff, but she had all these books around. And she was a huge fan of science fiction and horror culture. She ended up going back and finishing up later, but what ended up happening was that I was exposed to all these wild books that she was really into. So I started reading science fiction and fantasy super early. And I grew up in the sticks in rural Mississippi. You know she and my grandmother were my two major influences. My grandfather as well in some ways, like his work ethic. He just worked a lot and loved me. But my grandmother also had all these kinds of sayings and belief structures that I think, now looking back, was connected to hoodoo culture, conjure culture. So on one side I'm getting these ghost stories, stories about haints and superstitions and hexes, and I'm also reading Edgar Allan Poe and Stephen King. So I'm getting both of these things at the same time and this is what happens, when it happens. [laughs]

FHW: It's funny; I was raised primarily by my mother and grandmother as well. My mother had more the voodoo issues like to be able to read runes, did the astrological charts. But what I didn't have so much—I had the Roman Catholic upbringing as well—is basically what I consider one of the last polytheistic religions around. We got saints; we got demons.
JJ: And so many other religions hide in it because that's how slaves actually brought voodoo over was in Catholicism.

FHW: So if you're Roman Catholic you'd open yourself to all sorts of stories of monsters and wonderful things. And also what I think is interesting about your upbringing is that growing up in Mississippi—Mississippi is one of those places, for the few times I've visited, kind of like Ireland in the sense that you feel that magic exists there.
JJ: That's something—there's something in the air. It's either mystical, it's either scary, or it's powerful. There's a lot of creative people who come from Mississippi, like Elvis Presley and Oprah Winfrey. We wouldn't even have the Muppets without Mississippi. Jim Henson was from Mississippi. So it has a sense of longing and pain in it too. I was thinking about—I co-created this symposium because that's what I do in my spare time, [laughs] create

symposia. It was called Planet Deep South. So me and my friend Rego Chapman, we're going to do another one in Atlanta, looking at the fact that a lot of these ideas that come out of black speculative culture come out of the South. George Clinton was from the South. Sun Ra was from the South. Janelle Monae is actually based in the South. Dr. Martin Luther King Jr. talking about the mountaintop, that doesn't exist on this planet. He's dreaming up a space. He's thinking about the future; he's Afrofuture. So you think about anybody that's looking at revolutionary thought about where black people can go in the future I would consider having an Afrofuturist bent. They're coming out of the South, and they're creating these stories for us to follow. Someone like John A. Williams, who wrote this book *Captain Blackman*. He died a few months before we did this in Mississippi. This brother was from Mississippi, he was one of the black artists' movement, and he wrote science-fiction stories. *Captain Blackman* is a time-travel story. It's about a black soldier who's headed to Vietnam whose consciousness jumps through different time zones and into different black soldiers' bodies. So it becomes a critique about how black people are treated in the military.

FHW: That's what speculative fiction is for.
JJ: Right, exactly. You know I need to get the rights to that.

FHW: My last question, then I'm going to let you go after that. It kind of ties into that a little bit too. Going back to your *Uncaged* exhibit, which gave me a lot of stuff to think about.
JJ: You know it's a syllabus right? That's another thing it's a class.

FHW: It's a class. Yeah, I was wondering about it because it was split up like that. I wasn't sure.
JJ: It's a ten-week class. It's a class masquerading as an exhibition. That's why we call it an "Illabus." It's an illustrated syllabus. So you have the ten-week prompts, and you also have a bibliography of the books. Those are your reading lessons. And then if you read the images like text as well, you actually have a body of work to talk about. That's a class.

FHW: I was wondering about that because it was worded like a class, but I didn't know that. I just thought that was the conceit that was used for the purpose of the exhibit.
JJ: It's meant to be taken away and to be taught.

FHW: One of the other things I've read, which brought me to Afrofuturism, was the notion of Harlem. And Harlem as a utopia, which a lot of people—for me being a white guy, Harlem is not seen as being a black utopia.
JJ: Not these days.

FHW: Definitely not these days. If you think about it the days when everybody went to the clubs, had to go through [inaudible] in the Harlem Renaissance, people forget that was . . .
JJ: It's mecca. You had some of the most passionate, powerful, smartest black folk working in one space—Zora Neale Hurston, Langston Hughes, Countee Cullen, W. E. B. Du Bois, Aaron Douglas, Richmond Barthé, it just goes on and on. The Harlem Renaissance was a real thing. A lot of it being funded by some independent, wealthy white people actually. People like Charlotte [Osgood] Mason, for instance, was a huge donor to a lot of different folks. But it was a special place back then. It had its heyday; it had this special connection to black culture that I think it still to this day has, this kind of magical resonance,

FHW: Oh, I think it definitely does, especially when people start to look at the history of it and, even now in the archives, how it's a part of the city that's coming back, just like all parts of cities do. But whenever the notion of utopia is mentioned—or the word "utopia"—I automatically go to science fiction as futurism.
JJ: Yeah. You know, it's funny, and I've talked to my friend Stacey [Robinson] about this quite a bit because I don't think utopia is as possible as this idea of a perfect place because utopia means no place. It literally means no place. It's an imaginary space. I like the idea of a heterotopia. If you look at [Michel] Foucault's work *Of Other Spaces*, I think Harlem—because when you think of other space, then you think of different rules and regulations that give you a particular narrative on how to behave in that space and how they exist within other in-nested spaces. Heterotopia is like a space that exists within or inside of a real world. He gave examples like cemeteries and boys' homes where you have these different ways of getting into a space, and it has all these different rules and regulations. I look at those as being very interesting. Utopia as a notion is something that we try to aspire to. And for a while it was a perfect place where you're talking about people coming from all over the country to come to Harlem and try to make it there.

FHW: Well yes, it was a center for art and culture at that time. This is me making the pop culture reference, geeky thing, but now with this notion of

Wakanda as depicted in the movie *Black Panther* and the notion of Harlem in the Harlem Renaissance . . .
JJ: They start to resonate a little bit, don't they? Even to take it to another level because of the black laws and Jim Crow laws, black people were not allowed to participate in white culture at all. So my ancestors, a lot of us created black towns or black cities and black suburbs that in the early twentieth-century were destroyed by race riots and such. Back in the day a race riot used to be really angry racist white people destroying black towns. For instance, when you see the destruction of Black Wall Street in Tulsa, that was 1923 [1921]. We're talking about six black millionaires living in this space in Greenwood. So this was a massive destruction of a black space—they say you can't live here with us, so these people, they create their own space. And they're very successful, and it's destroyed. It's bombed from the sky. You know that's Wakanda.

FHW: Or what Wakanda is about to become when they open their borders, which is going to be interesting where that story goes. What's going to happen to this utopian society that's more advanced than anyplace else on earth now that they've opened their borders to all the corrupted areas around them?
JJ: Well, it makes sense that it would be. The thing about Wakanda to me is that it didn't make sense that it would exist in Africa because the countries in Africa don't function that way. They don't close their borders; they're not like Japan.

FHW: For people who think Africa is a country . . . [laughs]
JJ: Exactly. You see, Wakanda if it existed would probably be doing a lot of open trade. They wouldn't close itself off like that. That's one of the things it doesn't make sense to me about it, but we don't have to go into that. That's a whole other episode.

FHW: I thank you again. This has been fascinating. I really do hope this sparks some people's creative minds to start thinking in new areas and thinking outside the usual boxes because I think of the wealth waiting to be had from these stories. Again cheers.
JJ: Oh, thank you, appreciate it.

FHW: And that's a wrap on another episode of *Film Sense* . . . I'd like to thank our guest Professor John Jennings. This episode was recorded at the University of California, Riverside . . . produced by me Frank H. Woodward.

John Jennings Interview

DONNA-LYN WASHINGTON / 2019

Printed by permission of the editor and John Jennings.

Donna-lyn Washington: How did you get started in comics?
John Jennings: My mother bought me my first comics at a fairly young age. I fell in love with the medium almost immediately. When I saw the stories, the characters, and the colors in play, I was totally smitten by the form. I began my career in comics as a curator, editor, and scholar. Over the last twelve years, I have dedicated a great deal of creative energy and time to studying comics and making them. This has included editing scholarly works on comics, curating shows on comics, and designing and implementing pedagogy around comics.

DW: What forms of literature have influenced you as an educator?
JJ: My main influences from literature besides comics are various types of genre fiction such as horror, science fiction, mystery, and fantasy. I am also very influenced by mythology and folk legends.

DW: How important is it to have black representation in comics?
JJ: I think that black representation in all media is important. It's extremely important for all people who participate in this society to see themselves reflected in the culture. Studies have shown that when individuals don't see themselves as heroes in the stories they consume that it undermines their self-esteem. Also, there needs to be equity in representation to educate everyone about how to see their fellow man as human and not as stereotypes.

DW: You've used a mixture of genres in innovative ways. What impact do you want to convey through your graphic novels?
JJ: My training is as a graphic designer and design historian. So I have been thinking a great deal in recent years about race as a designed system and how

design epistemology can give us some insight around race and its associated graphic indexes. I have come up with a theoretical framework called critical race design studies. One aspect of this framing is to utilize designed narratives and illustrations to realign how the black subject is viewed and consumed. I create stories about black protagonists, create comics expos that feature black creators, and postulate positive futures for black people in order to redesign how black images are experienced. I want my books to extrapolate how the black experience is myriad and nuanced. I want to explore our humanity in my work.

DW: What are the challenges of adapting works that are not of your own creation?
JJ: The challenges are varied depending upon what you are adapting and the form that it takes. So one obvious aspect is format. Adapting *Kindred*, for instance, had a particular set of problems because of the fact that the original book is longer than the amount of pages we had allotted for the graphic novel. The other thing is that you can have more imagery in text and have hundreds of images on one page. Translation of one medium to the other is very complicated because each medium has different affordances.

DW: Your work is well researched. How would you describe your process in researching material for your work?
JJ: My process is very exacting. Once I begin working on something I want to know everything about the subject so that the audience is immersed within the world. It's part of the writing process. If the world doesn't feel complete, it disrupts the experience for the audience.

DW: I see speculative fiction and magical realism in your work. How would you describe the different forms of your craft?
JJ: The space I work in currently is what I call the Ethno-Gothic. It is a storytelling space posited by myself and Dr. Stanford Carpenter. "The Ethno-Gothic centers racially oriented speculative narratives that actively engage affective racialized psychological traumas via the traditions of gothic tropes and technologies. These tropes include the grotesque Other, body horror, haunted spaces, the hungry ghost, the uncanny, the doppelgänger, and multivalent disruptive tensions between the constructions of memory, history, the present, and the self."

DW: What do you think of Afrofuturism as a literary genre?

JJ: I think that Afrofuturism is a very interesting and culturally significant method for telling stories. It's not just a literary genre. It's a whole way of seeing and making that encompasses all of the arts. I do have to admit, however, that it simplifies the culture to just place everything that deals with blackness and speculative culture under one niche area. Afrofuturism isn't varied enough to deal with all of the nuances of black expressions in the speculative. I would actually think of it as a cultural production method and not necessarily a genre per se. For instance, is *Kindred* Afrofuturist? It's not about the future. It doesn't employ any futuristic technology that is alluded to by Mark Dery's definition. Octavia Butler's time-travel narrative actually has more akin to gothic horror. It's one of the reasons why the Ethno-Gothic emerged from my conversations with Dr. Carpenter. We were trying to negotiate the tensions between genre and production aesthetics.

DW: Have you ever used comic books/graphic novels in your teaching? Why or why not?
JJ: I actually teach entire courses centered around comics and graphic novels as literature. I have taught courses and workshops that center around making comics. I have taught these courses on both grad level and undergrad.

DW: If there was a comic book or graphic novel adapted from a novel you use in class would you assign it instead of a traditional novel?
JJ: I would either assign it or assign both and do a discussion about the affordances of text and comics.

DW: I've seen the call for papers for new essays to be added to the Eisner Award–winning *The Blacker the Ink: Constructions of Black Identity in Comics and Sequential Art*. What brought about the idea, and do you see this text as a living one where there will be additions in the future?
JJ: The initial idea came from myself and Damian Duffy. We wanted to extend our curatorial work into this academic space. I was still at UIUC and so was Damian and Frances Gateward. We pitched the idea to Frances, and she became an editor on the book. She is amazing and was such a boon to the project. Damian ended up having to step away from the project due to his acceptance into graduate school, and so Frances and I pushed forward on the book. I think we have thought about doing various aspects of the book as a follow up. We have thought about doing a totally new collection and also a collection of edited interviews. So I think that it is a living project because the scope of black comics has changed so much since we started the work. I hate that the

three of us couldn't have worked on the book, but Frances is a superstar and just really made the project shine.

DW: With your love and interest in horror movies, I'd like to know how the movie *Us* has informed your work.
JJ: I think that *Us* hasn't so much informed my work as validated it. When I see Jordan Peele's work and other creators of color making horror narratives, I can see the reflection of ideas that I have been talking about for the last few years staring back at me. It's almost like their work is the doppelgänger of mine.

DW: Also, considering the ideas of *Us* referring to the title of the film to mean the United States, the scenes that show classicism, the loss of voice, do you feel a personal connection with the themes in the film?
JJ: I think that the allegorical aspects of *Us* are just amazingly complex, and I feel a deep connection to what Peele was getting at with the use of the tethers. The really strong symbolism around how we perceive the Other and how that othered being really is born from and connected to us is an obvious truth that we constantly forget. I am working on a new project that has a similar idea at the center of it. It's a world I am building called the Inner Dark mythos that is a direct critique of H. P. Lovecraft's work.

DW: Seeing the artwork you've done based on the films *Get Out* and *Us* are you itching to do a solo project—a solo project with horror and classism themes, maybe a sequel to *Blue Hand Mojo*, or one with a set of new characters?
JJ: I am itching and scratching! I am totally embarrassed to say how many projects I have in development right now. I am definitely working on a follow up to *Blue Hand Mojo: Hard Times Road* and plan to put it out on my own imprint. I am also working on a bunch of collaborative projects that I am hoping to get out in the next two to three years.

DW: How would you envision an animated horror movie, not anything based on existing work, rather something where you see a void in horror today? And do you see the graphic novel *Kindred* getting the animated miniseries treatment?
JJ: I am a big fan of the type of animation used on the *Spawn* cartoon that was out on HBO in the late nineties. I think it really captured the dread in the comic, and I'd love to see something of that quality again in the market. There's never enough diversity in the animated space, and some horror stories

based on black writers' work could be really awesome. Victor LaValle's *Destroyer* would be a great cartoon! Or the works of Eden Royce of Tananarive Due as an anthology could be great. As for *Kindred*, I think I can see that working too, but I think a live action Netflix series would be best for it.

DW: You've mentioned the importance of the use of the term "megascope" for the name of your imprint for Abrams ComicArts. Having been an early incarnation for the title of Du Bois's short story "The Princess Steel," what connection do you feel with the megascope and how it's used in the story?
JJ: DuBois uses the device in "The Princess Steel" to frame the science fiction–fantasy allegory he deploys in the story. The megascope is a device created by the scientist in the story that can see through time and space and into seemingly parallel worlds. I just thought it was a wonderful way to create this story and that it would be a great name for my imprint. Also, I have been sort of obsessed with reclaiming black speculative artifacts from black narratives and normalizing them by using them in new stories. The megascope was a hidden gift that Du Bois left for us. So just as the *Necronomicon* is part of HP Lovecraft's legacy, this is Du Bois's contribution to weird fiction. I am in love with the idea of diegetic prototypes and design fictions. Du Bois and other writers have left us these wonderful inventions that we should really keep alive.

DW: Having recently reread Octavia Butler's prophetic *The Parable of the Sower*, what brought you and Damian Duffy to adapt it as a graphic novel?
JJ: After the success of *Kindred*, we were asked what other stories we would like to do. Despite the painful prescience of the Parable duology, we felt it was almost our duty to bring it to the illustrated page. *Parable of the Sower* and *Parable of the Talents* could happen tomorrow. They are all-too-real reminders of just how close we are to dystopia in this current political climate in our country. It's been painful to make, but we feel that these books were very important and needed to be done.

DW: Do you see *Sower* as a continuation to the themes in yours' and Duffy's graphic novel adaptation of *Kindred*?
JJ: I see them as continuations simply because they are of Butler's oeuvre. Octavia Butler wrote about the complex relationships around access to power and the overpowering need for humans to survive at any cost. So I think it's less with how we are seeing things and more about us picking up the threads of Butler as an author that she's already left for us.

DW: How did your collaboration with the creators of the comic-book series *Bitter Root* come about?
JJ: I am very good friends with David F. Walker, and once he told me what the story was I almost begged to be on the project! The themes were so close to my own research interests that I couldn't believe it! So, I signed on to do the editing and design of the back matter in *Bitter Root*. I even named the back matter as well: "Bitter Truths." I have been honored to work on that project, and I hope that I've made it a stronger book.

DW: Do you see your contribution to *Bitter Root* as exemplifying what Sankofa is able to do? And do you feel a connection to where you grew up?
JJ: I definitely feel a strong connection to the South in the book and also with the notions of how conjure is illustrated in the story. I do think that what I call "sankofarration" is apparent in the narrative as well. The creators are also very concerned with bringing these historicals full circle and representing them to new audiences. I am elated that the book has been so well received and is now nominated for an Eisner Award for Best New Series.

DW: I ask because I see a bit of Ma Etta in my own Grenadian grandmother on my mother's side and the stories of my Trinidadian great-grandmother on my father's. Do you see the characters in *Bitter Root* as a way of honoring root-working and possibly the ignorance or, rather, the impatience of the young?
JJ: I do think that there is a deep respect for root work in the story. Chuck [Brown] and David do a great job of dealing with the tensions of the modern with the old. I love the interplay of contemporary technology with root work. I came up with this term "ConjurePunk" to describe that tension and posit that it's a way to merge the old and new, the traditional and the modern.

DW: I know that you're on the editorial advisory board still; what brought on your collaboration with *New Suns: Race, Gender, and Sexuality in the Speculative* edited by Susan M. Morris and Kinitra D. Brooks? And how long have you been involved?
JJ: I have been involved since the beginning. I am very close friends with both Susanna and Kinitra, and Black Kirby (Stacey Robinson and myself) is designer for all of the covers for New Suns. I also helped name the series.

DW: This is a completely unfair question, but with *Avengers: Endgame* bringing this phase of the Marvel cinematic universe to a close, what are your favorite

Watson and Holmes. © 2019 John Jennings, permission of John Jennings.

films from the past ten years? Or what are your favorite scenes? Equally as important, what artwork would you like to have done?
JJ: My favorite Marvel film is still *The Winter Solider* [*Captain America*]. I think that it is such a great spy film! I loved *Black Panther*, of course. I also loved *Thor: Ragnarok*. I thought it totally captured the insanity of Thor's world. I also really loved the Ant-Man films. I think that *Endgame* was an amazing capstone to the last decade, but the solo films have always been my favorites. Although it's not the strongest of the films, I feel that I would have loved to have worked on *Doctor Strange*. He's one of my favorite Marvel characters. As an aside, Strange was designed by a Latina designer! How cool is that?

DW: Your collaboration with Stacey Robinson as Black Kirby is one of the projects that introduced me to your work as an educator and artist. Also, the recent edition of *Black Comix Returns* helped me find new writers and artists in the independent comics category. Who do you believe is underrated in today's comic-book market who didn't make it into *Returns* or in general?
JJ: I think that Jimmie Robinson is a brilliant creator, and I hate that we couldn't get work in time for *Black Comix Returns*. The same with Jennifer Crute. She is a brilliant woman, and I love her work. I would have also loved to have featured Rob Guilroy's work in *Black Comix*, and I want to see more work from Masheka Wood just in general.

DW: One of my favorite scenes from *Captain America: The Winter Soldier* is when Sam Wilson asks Steve Rogers (Captain America) what makes him happy. It's one of the few times Steve is seen as a person with dreams and feelings instead of a super-soldier. What brings you joy?
JJ: The fact that I am about to be a dad in a few weeks. I've been blessed to do the work that I do, but I think that the challenge of being a good father is the task I am most excited about.

INDEX

ABOUT THE EDITOR

Photo credit: Donna-lyn Washington

Donna-lyn Washington is English adjunct lecturer at Kingsborough Community College in Brooklyn, New York. She is also senior editor and senior writer at ReviewFix. She has contributed to *Reconsidering Frank Yerby: Critical Essays*, an academic anthology where her essay focuses on Yerby's readership and has contributed entries to the *Encyclopedia of Black Comics*.

Printed in the United States
By Bookmasters